Theory

of

Financial Markets

PRENTICE-HALL INTERNATIONAL SERIES IN MANAGEMENT

THEORY

OF

FINANCIAL MARKETS

JAN MOSSIN

Norwegian School of Economics
and Business Administration

PRENTICE-HALL, INC., Englewood Cliffs, New Jersey

Library of Congress Cataloging in Publication Data

MOSSIN, JAN.
 Theory of financial markets.

 (Prentice-Hall international series in management)
 Includes bibliograhpies.
 1. Corporation—Finance. I. Title.
HG4011. M568   332.6   72–2062
ISBN 0-13-913699-1

Printed in the United States of America

10   9   8   7   6   5   4   3   2   1

PRENTICE-HALL INTERNATIONAL, INC., *London*
PRENTICE-HALL OF AUSTRALIA, PTY. LTD., *Sydney*
PRENTICE-HALL OF CANADA, LTD., *Toronto*
PRENTICE-HALL OF INDIA PRIVATE LIMITED, *New Delhi*
PRENTICE-HALL OF JAPAN, INC., *Tokyo*

"To understand uncertainty and risk is
to understand the key business problem—
and the key business opportunity".

DAVID B. HERTZ

Contents

Preface

In this book I have attempted to describe a theoretical foundation for the analysis of the valuation of securities, the financing and investment decisions of the firm, and the efficiency of competitive markets in distributing investment capital among firms and in allocating the risk of return from investment among individuals. During the past several years a number of people have contributed to the formulation and analysis of these problems, and I feel that we now have at hand a reasonably unified and intellectually satisfactory theoretical framework for this class of economic phenomena.

There will no doubt be many who find a book like this rather too "theoretical" and abstract, and I shall be the first to admit that the investor looking for a foolproof way of making a killing in the stock market, or the corporate financial manager seeking a simple recipe for selecting among risky investment proposals, is well advised to look elsewhere (although I could not tell him where). I believe, however, that each should be able to approach his problem more soberly, and perhaps even more effectively, by seeing it in the perspective provided by a coherent theoretical framework.

Such a perspective is helpful in seeing where a particular problem fits in, how it is related to other problems, and what the most relevant variables affecting the problem may be. In many cases, theoretical considerations provide restrictions on both decision variables and exogenous variables which can narrow down the search for optimal decisions. A number of theoretical results presented in this book are essentially negative in character, asserting that certain things are not generally true or that certain relationships do not generally hold. Such results may serve as checks on the consistency and appropriateness of various "rules of thumb" or expressions of conventional wisdom in the area. Even when certain implications of a theoretical model are clearly contradicted by observation, the theoretical framework should not be dismissed as useless. Unless we have made a logical error, such a contradiction can occur only because some of the assumptions on which the model is based are not satisfied in practice. By examining these assumptions we shall often be able to find precisely what is being violated, and thus be able to evaluate the nature and significance of the discrepancy.

In form and style this book may perhaps look more like a monograph than a textbook. It is based, however, on lecture notes from courses I gave in the Graduate School of Business Administration at the University of California, Berkeley, during my visit there in 1969–1970, and has been written with a view to the need for a text of a particular kind. There now seems to be a trend towards organizing more advanced graduate courses around a relatively concise "core" text, with readings being liberally supplemented from other sources, mainly journal articles. This gives the instructor great flexibility in structuring his course so as to emphasize and expand on those topics he considers most relevant, while maintaining a degree of unity and perspective. As a textbook of this kind, its coverage should find application in both graduate business administration and economics curricula.

I shall not comment here in any detail on the organization of the book, since Chapter I goes into this more thoroughly. Suffice it to say that the book follows a definite sequence of development in which one chapter builds directly on material covered in the preceding ones. I think it is important to have a clear idea of this sequence of development before embarking on a detailed reading, and it is for this reason that I have found it fitting to give an introductory précis in Chapter I. My only advice is therefore to read Chapter I carefully in order to get an appreciation of what follows. This chapter may also be useful as a reference and summary during or after reading the book.

It should be possible to follow the main line of argument in this book without much technical knowledge of advanced mathematics. However, in order to understand an argument more completely and to use and evaluate it critically, a reasonably good background in quantitative methods is required. This would include a fair amount of calculus, including partial derivatives, Lagrange multipliers, and occasionally some knowledge of elementary differential equations; some elementary linear algebra; and familiarity with the basic concepts of probability and statistics. This is not to say that anyone with a course coverage of these topics will find the book suitable for bedside reading. So far as studying mathematical economics is concerned, I am a firm believer in the straight wooden chair and the pad and pencil beside the book. All derivations should be retraced in detail, and nothing the author says (such as "it is easily verified that") should be taken at face value.

I should like to express my grateful thanks to the following friends and colleagues who have kindly read and criticized earlier drafts of the manuscript: S. H. Archer, K. H. Borch, K. P. Hagen, N. H. Hakansson, J. Hirshleifer, D. H. Pyle, and A. Sandmo.

JAN MOSSIN

Theory

of

Financial Markets

1 Introduction

and Overview of the Book

1.1. The theory of finance has—or should have—two principal objectives. The theory should be able to explain and interpret phenomena in financial markets. It should also be able to assist management in formulating a company's financial policy by providing useful analytical tools within a realistic theoretical framework.

These two aspects of the theory of finance are closely related for a very simple reason. The most universally accepted formulation of company objectives is maximization of the market value of the company's equity. Through its actions management can *influence* the market value, but is clearly unable to *determine* it completely. Market value is determined by the simultaneous interplay of supply and demand in the security markets, where other companies also participate as suppliers of securities, and a great number of *investors* participate in the demand for these securities. No theory of finance can give a satisfactory explanation of security valuation or investment behavior if it fails to take into account relationships among individual investors' portfolio decisions. This means that all the investment alternatives open to the investor must be considered if we want to understand his evaluation of any one of them. Market values are determined by the demands of all investors, and this leads us to study the theory of *general equilibrium* in competitive security markets. Without such a model we are unable to foresee the effects of corporate investment and financing decisions. But once we have a theory of share valuation, we also have in hand a theory of optimal financing and investment decisions.

1.2.   In view of the fundamental theoretical role that analysis of security markets should play in the study of corporate decisions, it is remarkable to what limited extent such an analysis has been brought into existing financial literature. Without going into a review of the literature, I think it is fair to say that the market plays a highly indirect role in most discussions of share valuation. A number of hypotheses are advanced concerning the way in which the market evaluates and reacts (e.g., with respect to discounting for time and uncertainty), but these are usually ad hoc and rather arbitrary, since they are not *derived* from any fundamental assumptions describing market equilibrium. Financial theory seems to have been lacking a reasonably satisfactory theoretical foundation.

The objective of this book is to develop, as carefully as possible, just such a theoretical framework. In the light of some recent contributions to the theory of security market equilibrium, we are now, I feel, in a position to provide a reasonably unified and coherent development of a theory of security valuation and its implications for the analysis of a firm's investment and financing decisions. Let us consider, in broad outline, how such a development would proceed.

1.3.   Clearly, to construct a general equilibrium model, we need to specify investors' demand for the various securities available. This is the same as specifying the quantities they would buy of the various securities, given the total amount of money they want to spend, the yield characteristics of the securities, and their prices. This is referred to as the portfolio selection problem, and a rather extensive literature exists about it.

Since portfolio selection represents an application of the theory of decision making under uncertainty, it seems appropriate to start our development with a presentation of that theory. It would be outside the scope of this book to give a complete account of the theory of decision making under uncertainty, but in Chapter II we do discuss some selected aspects of it. First, there are a number of general concepts and ideas that will be useful throughout the book. Second, I have tried to put the theory in its proper perspective by emphasizing its purpose, its usefulness, and its possible applications, rather than spending most of the effort on such technicalities as proving the expected utility theorem.

Thus armed, Chapter III contains an account of some different approaches to the theory of portfolio selection. As noted, the purpose is to specify the demand side of the securities market, so we are not concerned with portfolio selection as an end in itself, but rather as a link in the development of a theory of financial markets. Although we do not entirely disregard problems of operationality, we brush aside a number of practical details.

1.4. The next step is to inquire into the characteristics of the whole market for securities when individual demands are interacting to determine the prices and allocation of the existing supply of securities among investors. The model we present in Chapter IV is actually very much in the classical tradition. Formally, it is a model of pure exchange, and there are two types of exchange objects: bonds, issued either by firms or by investors themselves, and ordinary corporate shares. Being a model of pure exchange, it takes as given the firms' investment and financing decisions: on the basis of relationships to be derived between these decisions and market value, we can infer the effects of *alternative* decisions. (Later, in Chapter VIII, we consider the problems concerned with determination of the overall level of activity of the firm.)

The equilibrium solution has several interesting properties which will be discussed and interpreted. Probably the most important result is the derivation of a *market valuation formula:* an explicit expression for the value of the firm in terms of characteristics of the probability distribution for its earnings and other market parameters. This market valuation formula obviously plays a most important role in the subsequent analysis of optimal financial policies for the firm.

The equilibrium model as initially presented rests on a number of assumptions, with respect both to investors' preferences and the nature of their environment. Some of these may seem quite restrictive, and it is obviously necessary to know more about their importance, that is, to see whether the results of Chapter IV are seriously affected by a relaxation of the assumptions. Chapter V examines some of the most important (or objectionable) ones. Specifically, we show that the Modigliani-Miller proposition on the basic irrelevance of debt level for company valuation holds under extremely general conditions, and that, although to a lesser extent, the validity of the market valuation formula is quite robust with respect to the model's underlying assumptions. The overall conclusion is therefore that these assumptions do not appear to be unduly restrictive. Their main purpose can be seen as simplifying the analysis without seriously affecting the generality of our results.

1.5. How do financial markets perform their job? In the traditional Walras model of equilibrium in commodity markets, one of the central results is that a competitive equilibrium leads to an efficient, or Pareto-optimal, allocation of commodities. That is, if consumers take their income and the market prices as given data and trade at these prices, the resulting allocation is such that it is impossible to find a reallocation which makes some consumers better off without making others worse off. This result, which is of fundamental importance in economic theory, does not necessarily hold when uncertainty is introduced.

The precise meaning and implications of this statement are elaborated in Chapter VI. We start with a general discussion of the concept of

Pareto optimality, and then show that a market for bonds and ordinary shares is in general able to achieve only a *constrained* Pareto optimum. The constraint arises because ordinary shares give the owner only a proportional interest in a company, whereas some nonproportional scheme (or "sharing rule") might actually be preferable. Examination shows that Pareto-optimal sharing rules can be effected by means of markets for stocks and bonds (or other familiar securities) only under rather restrictive assumptions about investors' preferences. The question then arises as to whether it is possible to save the central result of classical equilibrium theory by introducing markets for securities different from those to which we are accustomed. The answer is a qualified yes: we can conceive of securities that "in theory" would do the job, but since in principle this would require an infinite number of different kinds of securities, it is difficult to see how such a system might be implemented. However, the idea that creation of new kinds of securities may serve to increase the efficiency of financial markets does provide interesting sidelights on certain observable capital market phenomena.

1.6. Chapter VI may be considered a digression (although an important one) from the main line of argument of the book. In Chapter VII we return to the stock market model developed earlier in order to examine its implications for the analysis of corporate financial policy. I think it is fair to say that our approach serves both to clarify and extend traditional financial theory, and to bring out certain misconceptions in that theory. We start with a critical assessment of the Modigliani-Miller investment theory and point out its limited scope and approximate nature. We then show that, by means of our market valuations model, we can extend the investment analysis to projects with completely arbitrary return characteristics (not only "nondiversifying" projects). As special cases, we consider investment criteria for riskless investments and investment criteria in the presence of default risk. On the basis of this analysis we examine the cost of capital concept and argue that only in special cases does such a concept seem useful or even meaningful. We conclude the discussion of investment theory by comparing investment criteria for different firms and examining certain "externality" aspects of risky investments. In the last part of the chapter we discuss some possible approaches to the dividend decision in the context of our market valuation model, describe the nature of the problems involved in constructing a general dividend theory, and indicate some alternative approaches.

1.7. Even though the theory presented up to this point provides a number of useful insights, it is still basically partial in nature. It offers no real explanation of how or why companies have arrived at their yield distribution and amount of debt. Rather, we analyze *marginal* changes in company investment activity. Clearly, there must be some discretion involved in the relationship between the liability side of the firm's balance sheet and the yield made possible by the corresponding resources on the asset side. Chapter VIII discusses the nature of the problems involved in such an extension of the theory to include the simultaneous determination of the distribution of total investment capital among firms and the allocation of claims to the resulting output among investors. It is difficult to paraphrase the results of this analysis in a compact way, but the character of the market allocation is radically different depending on whether investment is debt financed or includes equity financing ("initial financing"). The former case allows a relatively problem-free extension of the analysis of Chapter VII, while the latter situation poses rather intricate problems. At the heart of the problem seems to lie a certain kind of circularity among variables which prevents us from a meaningful formulation of company objectives.

2 Risk Taking

and Risk Aversion

2.1. In this chapter we shall discuss and attempt to clarify certain issues and problems in the theory of decision making under uncertainty. Most students in economics or business administration have been introduced to this theory, so the purpose of the following presentation is not to give a detailed presentation of its formal aspects, but rather to illustrate its interpretation and application in various decision-making situations. The main tool in the analysis of such decisions, the so-called *expected utility theorem*, is useful, even indispensable, but ultimately no more than a tool. Our primary interest must be in knowing how to handle it.

2.2. To begin with, let us make clear what the theory of decision making under uncertainty is all about. Its purpose is to explain people's choices among alternative courses of action in situations where an action does not uniquely determine the outcome. This is the same as saying that the theory deals with *choices among probability distributions*. By choosing one action, we get one probability distribution; by choosing another, we get another. Thus, to make a decision under uncertainty consists in a choice of a probability distribution. When formulated in this way, the nature of the theory becomes clearer. We shall present several illustrations of this view of the theory below.

2.3.   The theory takes as point of departure the fact that people frequently make decisions under uncertainty, and therefore must be assumed to have certain preferences with respect to probability distributions. This should mean that a person presented with a list of specific probability distributions should be able to *rank* them in order of preference.

To proceed with the development of the theory we need to find a simple way of describing such preference rankings. Specification of a probability distribution can be fairly complicated, generally consisting of a two-column table—one for outcomes and one for corresponding probabilities. In order to facilitate comparisons, we would like to be able to assign to each probability distribution a number which we shall call a *preference index*.

Similar problems arise in many other areas of life. Let us consider one of the author's favorites: speed skating. A competitor's results during a match consist of four pairs of numbers, for example:

Distance	Time
500 m.	40.9
1500 m.	2,11.1
5000 m.	7,52.0
10000 m.	15,50.8

We find it natural and desirable to summarize such tables by computing a point value to characterize and compare the competitor's standing. We do this by assigning to each distance a *weight* (e.g., 1, 1/3, 1/10, 1/20) and then calculating a weighted sum of the times for each distance (here 179.54). If we denote the distances by d, the times by $t(d)$, and the weights $v(d)$, the point value is thus computed as $\sum_d v(d)t(d)$. There may be disagreement on the relative numerical values of the weights, but the general principle seems to be commonly accepted.

In the same way, we should like to summarize a probability distribution, for example:

y	$f(y)$
1000	0.1
1500	0.4
2000	0.3
2500	0.2

by a single number to indicate how well we like it. It is obvious that if this were possible, the analysis of preferences among probability distribution

would be much simpler, eliminating the need to study long lists of complicated specifications.

2.4.   This problem is precisely what is solved by the expected utility
theorem, which says that if a person satisfies certain simple rules of rational
behavior, then he may represent his preference ordering by such a simple
calculation of a point value. Just as for speed skating, the calculation requires
the specification of weights for each outcome, and then proceeds by computing the average (or expected) weight, using the probabilities of each outcome
in the usual way. That is: with each outcome Y is associated a weight $u(Y)$,
and the preference index for the probability distribution $f(y) = Pr[Y = y]$
is calculated as[1]

$$U(f) = \sum u(y)f(y).$$

If, in the example above, the weights were given by (0, .4, .7, 1.0), the preference index would be 0(.1) + .4(.4) + .7(.3) + 1.0(.2) = .57.

The *weight function* (i.e., the assignment of weights to outcomes)
which our person uses to describe his preferences is usually referred to as his
utility function. This function is not uniquely determined. We say that it is
determined only up to a positive linear transformation, by which we mean
that if some particular function $u(Y)$ can serve to describe a preference ordering, then so can any other function of the form $au(Y) + b$ (where a and b
are constants with $a > 0$). For speed skating we could also multiply the
weights by an arbitrary positive number; if all weights were doubled the point
values would be doubled, but this would not change the ranking of the
competitors. We could also add numbers to the *point values* without altering
the ranking; however, this *cannot* be achieved by adding arbitrary numbers
to the *weights:* e.g., the weights (19/20, 17/60, 1/20, 0) would invariably result
in a different ranking. This is so because in speed skating there is no constraint
on the times for the various distances, whereas for probability distributions
we know that the probabilities sum to unity. This means that

$$\sum_y [au(y) + b]f(y) = a \sum_y u(y)f(y) + b \sum_y f(y)$$

$$= a \sum_y u(y)f(y) + b,$$

while for speed skating we would have

$$\sum_d [av(d) + b]t(d) = a \sum_d v(d)t(d) + b \sum_d t(d),$$

---

[1]Throughout this book we shall write all probability distributions as discrete
functions. All results remain valid if summation is replaced by integration in the case of
continuous probability distributions.

and the latter sum is not the same in all cases. A utility function which is determined up to a linear transformation is referred to as a *cardinal* utility function.

2.5. In this connection, any "psychological" connotations of the term "utility function" for the weight function $u(Y)$ should be warned against. This term suggests reference to the weight associated with an outcome as the "utility" of that outcome, which in turn suggests an interpretation of utility as a psychological measure of "intensity of satisfaction" from obtaining the outcome. Such an interpretation is neither warranted nor necessary, and in most cases is misleading. All that the utility function is meant to do is to define a mapping from a set of probability distributions onto the real line. Introduction of the term "utility function" is an unfortunate historical accident.

The only merit of the expected utility theorem thus lies in the fact that it allows us to describe a preference ordering in a particularly simple and economical way. Confronted with any probability distribution, we can just insert our set of weights to get a single number which indicates its ranking on our valuation scale. Apart from this, the two methods for describing preferences are completely equivalent, and the expected utility theorem is therefore devoid of meaningful implications. That is, the expected utility theorem allows no hypotheses about a person's choices or behavior beyond what we may already know about the underlying preference ordering.

2.6. As stated earlier, the expected utility theorem itself is concerned with the conditions under which a preference ordering for probability distributions can be represented in the way we have described. If we cut through the various fine points and mathematical detail involved, we shall find that these conditions, although not entirely trivial, are not very demanding, particularly in view of many of the assumptions we make in other parts of economic theory. We shall not give a full treatment of the theorem, but just state the conditions informally and indicate the intuitive idea behind the theorem.

The most important condition is quite simply this: To any probability distribution there corresponds a value (called a *certainty equivalent*) which is such that the person is indifferent whether he gets the certainty equivalent or the probability distribution itself, and which furthermore is such that if he prefers probability distribution f_1 to probability distribution f_2, then the certainty equivalent of f_1 is preferred to that of f_2. This condition makes it possible to assign a number (a preference index) to any probability distribution. If the outcomes are amounts of money, the condition simply says that everything has its price, and things that have a price are what economics is mostly about.

The remaining conditions are required to specify a particular *method* for assigning values to probability distributions. The next condition can therefore be stated: If the person is indifferent between two probability distributions, he should not mind letting a chance mechanism (e.g., a coin toss) determine which one he gets. In other words, if two probability distributions f_1 and f_2 have the same certainty equivalent, then for any $\alpha\,(0 \le \alpha \le 1)$ the probability distribution $f = \alpha f_1 + (1 - \alpha)f_2$ has the same certainty equivalent. The condition itself amounts to little more than a reasonable interpretation of what we mean by "indifference."

We would finally need some kind of continuity assumption, and one way of formulating this is the following: If the probability of outcome a is p and that of b is $(1 - p)$, then (i) the certainty equivalent is a if $p = 1$ and b if $p = 0$, and (ii) the certainty equivalent is a continuous function of p as p varies between 0 and 1. We can say that this assumption rules out any kind of "superstition" with respect to particular probabilities.

The implications of the preceding conditions can be illustrated with the familiar technique of indifference curve analysis for the simplest possible case of preferences over three-point probability distributions (with fixed outcomes). Since the probabilities sum to one, it is in this case possible to represent a probability distribution by a point in the plane, with the probabilities for two of the outcomes along the axes. That is, suppose there are the three outcomes x_1, x_2, and x_3, with probabilities p_1, p_2, and $1 - p_1 - p_2$, respectively; then a probability distribution is represented by a point in the p_1, p_2 plane, and a preference ordering over such probability distributions can be represented by indifference curves in this plane. Figure 1 shows the representation of two such probability distributions, f_1 and f_2, given by

x	$f_1(x)$	x	$f_2(x)$
x_1	.30	x_1	.40
x_2	.50	x_2	.25
x_3	.20	x_3	.35

Assume now that our person is indifferent between these two distributions, which means that the points labeled f_1 and f_2 must lie on the same indifference curve. By our hypothesis, any mixed distribution of the type $f = \alpha f_1 + (1 - \alpha)f_2$ should also lie on the same indifference curve. The diagram shows the plotting of the distribution $f = .4f_1 + .6f_2$, which is given by

x	$f(x)$
x_1	.36
x_2	.35
x_3	.29

FIGURE 1

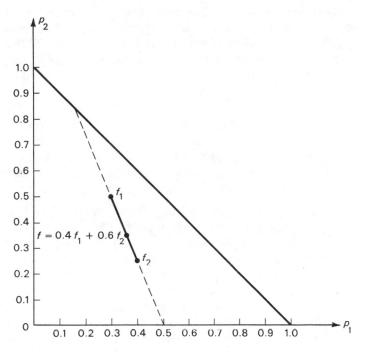

Clearly, all such distributions must be represented by points along the straight line between the points f_1 and f_2. In other words, the indifference curve joining the points f_1 and f_2 is a straight line. It now follows from the continuity assumption that the complete indifference map must consist of parallel straight lines. But then the "utility surface" above the p_1, p_2 plane must be a plane, i.e., given algebraically in the form

$$U(f) = a + b_1 p_1 + b_2 p_2$$

which then can be normalized to the form

$$U(f) = a_1 p_1 + a_2 p_2 + a_3 p_3.$$

Thus, quite generally, the conditions above imply that the preference index associated with any probability distribution is a weighted sum of the probabilities of the various outcomes:

$$U(f) = \sum_x u(x) f(x).$$

In our example it is clear that the weights must be given by $u(x_1) = 0$, $u(x_2) = .6$, $u(x_3) = 1$, or linear transformations of these numbers.

2.7.   Of course, we do not postulate that people who make decisions under uncertainty consciously think in terms of expected utility. Their method or "formula" for ranking alternative probability distributions may look like anything, and still be completely rational. However, if their decision rule cannot *alternatively* be stated in terms of expectation of a utility function, then that rule violates one or more of the rationality conditions stated above. We shall give some examples of such rules later.

It is noted that if our rationality conditions are accepted, the evaluation of a course of action can always be broken down into two separate sets of evaluations: evaluation of a set of weights for the outcomes and evaluation of a set of probabilities. This allows us to approach a decision problem in an orderly and systematic fashion. However, some comments on the assignment of probabilities are in order.

2.8.   When we describe decision making under uncertainty as a choice among probability distributions, we assume implicitly that the decision maker is able or willing to assign probabilities to the different outcomes which can result from his decision. Of course, there are many types of decisions in which the situation is so vague that an assignment of precise probabilities seems extremely difficult. This has led a number of theorists to attempts at establishing decision rules that do not make use of such probability assessments. These attempts would seem to be in line with the time-honored distinction (introduced by Knight [4]) between situations characterized by "risk" (known probabilities) and those characterized by "uncertainty" (unknown probabilities). We have not adopted this distinction, because even after 50 years' existence it seems to serve no useful theoretical or practical purpose. We shall paraphrase some of the argument.

First, the distinction is nonoperational, since it is logically next to impossible to give precise meaning to the statement that the probabilities are unknown. Further, if we insist that we are completely ignorant as to which outcome will occur, it is hard to escape the implication that all outcomes are equally probable. But this means that the probabilities have become known, making the distinction between risk and uncertainty unnecessary.

Second, complete ignorance about the chance mechanisms involved is probably no more typical than complete knowledge. If partial knowledge is admitted, the question is a matter of degree of confidence in probability assessments rather than one of dichotomy.

Third, if we do have some knowledge, no matter how vague, partial, or incomplete, it would be inefficient not to use it. A decision rule which does not make use of probabilities amounts to a waste of information.

Fourth, even though a decision rule may not take probability information explicitly into account, it will in many cases contain an *implicit* probability assignment to outcomes.

Fifth, but most important, the Savage theorem [7] completely obviates the need for distinction between, and separate theories of decision making for, situations of "risk" and "uncertainty." The Savage theorem can be considered as an extension of the expected utility theorem; it states that if certain consistency conditions are satisfied, then to any preference ordering of a set of actions with possible outcomes y there corresponds

1. A weight function $u(y)$ over the outcomes—unique up to a linear transformation;
2. A unique function $f(y)$ satisfying all the properties of a probability measure,

such that $\sum u(y)f(y)$ represents the ordering. In other words, *any* consistent decision rule can alternatively be formulated as expected utility maximization.

A kind of uncertainty which may be looked upon as significantly different from the kind we have considered is referred to as *game-theoretic* uncertainty, and can be described as uncertainty with respect to the actions of one or more intelligent opponents or competitors. The decision problems of such a situation are entirely different from those that arise when the uncertainty is due to impersonal factors such as weather, technology, market forces, or sheer lack of information, and therefore call for an approach radically different from the one we have used. There is no reason to expect that decision rules, such as the minimax rule, which are appropriate for game situations should be meaningful or relevant in nongame situations. Nevertheless, such ideas have not been uncommon in economic literature, despite the fact that the minimax or similar rules fail to explain observed behavior.

2.9. With these remarks, let us proceed to an examination of some typical decision problems under uncertainty. The simplest version of such a problem consists of the following elements:

1. The *outcome* in which we are interested, described by a random variable Y;
2. A *decision variable*, a, the value of which is to be chosen and which will influence the form of the probability distribution for the outcome Y;
3. A number of *exogenous variables*, W, which also affect the probability distribution for the outcome, but which lie beyond the decision maker's control.

Description of the decision problem now consists in specifying the set of probability distributions associated with the set of possible values of a and W, i.e., specifying the decision problem consists in specifying the set of probability distributions

$$f(y; a, W) = Pr\,[Y = y \,|\, a, W].$$

2.10.   A practical example which fits this general characterization is the simplest possible version of a *portfolio selection* problem. In this problem, we have a given amount of money W (initial wealth) which can be used for investment in two different assets. One of the assets is completely riskless but yields no return to the owner (we can think of it as "cash"). For the other asset, however, the return is stochastic—we shall assume that by the end of a certain period we have either lost everything we invested (a return of -1) with probability p, or we receive three dollars for every dollar invested (a return of $+2$). Thus, if we denote the return by X, the expected return is $\mathcal{E}(X) = p(-1) + (1-p)2 = 2 - 3p$. The *exogenous variables* are then W and p.

The *decision* to be made is the amount a to be invested in the risky asset. The *outcome* Y in which we are interested is the amount of money we have at the end of period (final wealth). The *probability distribution* for the outcome is generally specified as

y	$f(y)$
$W - a$	p
$W + 2a$	$1 - p$

If the values of p and W were taken as given, e.g., $p = 1/2$, $W = 1000$, we could now proceed to construct a sequence of specific probability distributions, one for each value of a. The following would be examples:

(a) $a = 0$		(b) $a = 200$		(c) $a = 600$	
y	$f(y)$	y	$f(y)$	y	$f(y)$
1000	1	800	1/2	400	1/2
		1400	1/2	2200	1/2

Our next step would be to rank these distributions according to how well we liked them; e.g., in the order b-a-c.

By means of the expected utility theorem, however, we can compute a preference index as an expected utility in the form

(1) $$U(a; W, p) = pu(W - a) + (1 - p)u(W + 2a).$$

Thus, for the three distributions above we get the indexes

(2a) $U(\ \ 0; 1000, \tfrac{1}{2}) = u(1000)$

(2b) $U(200; 1000, \tfrac{1}{2}) = \tfrac{1}{2}u(800) + \tfrac{1}{2}u(1400)$

(2c) $U(600; 1000, \tfrac{1}{2}) = \tfrac{1}{2}u(400) + \tfrac{1}{2}u(2200).$

If somehow we knew that the weight function was $u(Y) = \ln Y$, the preference indexes would be 6.91, 6.96, and 6.84, respectively. This is an alternative way of expressing the rank ordering b-a-c.

2.11. Perhaps a word is in order on the specification of the *argument* of the utility function. The expected utility theorem itself says nothing about what kinds of things the outcomes of a random event refer to; they may be anything from the length of time it takes to drive home to the amount of money to be made in the stock market. Actually, the theorem is easily generalized to handle combinations of several variables (apples and oranges, or consumption in several different periods), so expected utilities can be calculated for joint probability distributions for such variables.

In the portfolio selection problem we have assumed that the outcome of our decision is completely described by the level of final wealth, but there is nothing sacrosanct about this. Furthermore, as long as we take initial wealth as a given and constant datum, say 1000, we may express the level of wealth equally well by absolute or relative return; that is, a final wealth of 1200 may be expressed as an absolute return of 200 or a relative return of 20 per cent.

2.12. We pointed out earlier that the only purpose of the expected utility theorem is to allow preferences over probability distributions to be described in a concise and manageable way. There are still those who complain that, although there may be nothing wrong with the expected utility theorem, its usefulness is doubtful because we hardly ever know what people's utility functions look like. The preceding discussion should make clear the negativism of such a statement as "We can't say what people will do because we don't know what they want." Such thinking tends to obscure the problems that exist in decision theory. There is an obvious need for inferences on people's preferences from observation of their behavior in choice situations; it should be equally obvious that *it is the expected utility theorem that makes such inferences possible.* Without the expected utility theorem, any attempt at systematic analysis of decision making under uncertainty would be impossibly complicated.

How, then, is it possible to determine a weight (or utility) function which may represent the preference structure of a particular person? A relatively direct procedure is to offer him a series of binary choices (usually between a certain outcome and a two-point probability distribution). On the basis of his choices, we can determine points on the utility function representing the underlying preferences. Once the shape of this function is determined, we can predict his behavior in other situations, no matter how complicated, or we can give him advice on how he *should* behave.

Such a direct interview technique may seem both difficult and time-consuming. It may therefore be useful to observe people's behavior in more general terms and see the implications of this behavior for the form of the utility function. We can think of several ways of making such inferences.

2.13.   We might, for example, encounter a person who tells us that all he needs to know when making a decision under uncertainty is the mean E and the standard deviation S of the probability distribution for the outcome. If this is really the case, we can make rather specific conclusions about the utility function which represents his preferences. As we shall see, we then know that it must be quadratic, say:[2]

$$u(Y) = Y - cY^2.$$

In that case, the ranking criterion—expected utility—is given by[3]

$$\mathcal{E}[u(Y)] = E - c(E^2 + S^2).$$

We only need the value of the constant c, and it is easy to see that it can be determined if we know two points in the E, S plane which our person finds equally good.

2.14.   The task is not usually that easily carried out, and we have to take a more methodical approach. If the outcomes refer to amounts of money, we assume, for example, without much qualm, that the weight assigned to an outcome ("the utility of money") increases with the amount; this implies that $u(Y)$ is an increasing function: $u'(Y) > 0$.

Another important assumption which is commonly made is that behavior is characterized by something called *risk aversion*. In the case of a quadratic utility function, risk aversion would be present if $c > 0$; that is, a probability distribution ranks lower the larger the standard deviation (for a given mean). When we do not limit ourselves to considering mean and standard deviation only, the meaning of risk aversion is less clear-cut. What we have in mind, however, is that a certain outcome is preferred to a stochastic one with the same expected outcome. This suggests that we *define* risk aversion as unwillingness to engage in gambles with an expected outcome of zero (neutral, or fair, gambles). Thus, a person who declines a gamble in which he may win or lose an amount h with equal probability is by definition risk averse. If his present wealth is W, final wealth under such a prospect would have the probability distribution

y	$f(y)$
$W - h$	$1/2$
$W + h$	$1/2$

[2]Because of the nonuniqueness, there is no loss of generality in writing a quadratic utility function in this way; any second-degree polynomial is equivalent, as a utility function, to a function written in this form.

[3]Any statistics text shows that the variance of a variable Y can be computed as the expectation of the square of Y minus the square of the expectation of Y, i.e., $S^2 = \mathcal{E}(Y^2) - E^2$; hence $\mathcal{E}(Y^2) = E^2 + S^2$.

while if he declines it would be

y	$f(y)$
W	1

The two probability distributions have preference indexes (expected utilities) of $\frac{1}{2}u(W - h) + \frac{1}{2}u(W + h)$ and $u(W)$, respectively, and since he prefers the latter, u must be such that

$$u(W) > \tfrac{1}{2}u(W - h) + \tfrac{1}{2}u(W + h)$$

for any h. The inequality can be written

$$u(W) - u(W - h) > u(W + h) - u(W),$$

i.e., increases in u from equal increases in Y become successively smaller. This clearly implies that u is a *concave* function and therefore has the property that its second derivative is negative: $u''(Y) < 0$.

2.15.   We do not expect the assumption of risk aversion to hold for everyone under every circumstance; phenomena such as lotteries or Las Vegas cannot be explained without assuming that there are persons (or situations) not characterized by risk aversion. However, more prosaic phenomena, such as insurance companies or diversified portfolios, cannot be explained without the assumption of risk aversion. Risk aversion seems a reasonable assumption in the analysis of more ordinary business problems, and these are the problems with which we are concerned in this book.

Actually, the "paradox" represented by people who gamble and buy insurance at the same time does not seem particularly paradoxical, and attempts such as Friedman and Savage's [3] to explain such behavior in terms of a utility function for money alone do not make much sense. A person who buys a lottery ticket does not only buy a probability distribution for gains; he also buys something extra, "excitement," let us say. Thus, we are led to consider preferences over *pairs* of outcomes: money and excitement. Suppose I can buy a $1 lottery ticket from which I can win $1000 with a probability of .001. If I don't buy the ticket, my "excitement index" is zero, while if I do, it will be 1. Thus, in the former case, expected utility will be $u(W, 0)$; in the latter, $.999u(W - 1, 1) + .001u(W + 999, 1)$. It is obvious that the latter expression may be larger than the former, even though $\partial^2 u/\partial W^2 < 0$. The paradox lies not in the behavior, but in the theorist's improper specification of the arguments of my utility function.[4]

2.16.   Let us proceed with the analysis of our little portfolio problem. We had concluded that if W and p were given and we chose to invest the

---

[4]Another explanation of the phenomenon is that people tend to overestimate both the probabilities of winning in gambling situations and of being exposed to risk in insurance situations.

amount a, the probability distribution for final wealth would have a preference index as given by (1). The immediate problem is to characterize the optimal a in terms of this index.

The two first derivatives with respect to a are

$$\frac{dU}{da} = -pu'(W - a) + 2(1 - p)u'(W + 2a),$$

$$\frac{d^2U}{da^2} = pu''(W - a) + 4(1 - p)u''(W + 2a).$$

Since we assume risk aversion d^2U/da^2 must be negative, this means that U is a concave function of a, and hence a unique maximum exists.

Let us first consider the possibility that $a = 0$ is the optimal solution. This would be the case if the first derivative at this point were negative, i.e., if

$$\left.\frac{dU}{da}\right|_{a=0} = -pu'(W) + 2(1 - p)u'(W)$$

$$= u'(W)(2 - 3p)$$

$$= u'(W)\mathcal{E}(X) < 0.$$

Since $u' > 0$, this condition is satisfied if and only if the expected return $\mathcal{E}(X)$ is negative. Antithetically, the interpretation is that *something* will always be invested in the risky asset if its expected return is positive.

We observe that this conclusion is independent of any other assumption than $u' > 0$. (A person for whom $u'' > 0$ would obviously stake any feasible amount in the risky asset.) If, in spite of positive expected return, a person refused to invest in the risky asset, we should have to conclude that he behaved irrationally, in the sense that he did not satisfy the rationality conditions on which the expected utility representation is based (he would not have a complete preference ordering over probability distributions). We shall assume, however, that this is not the case.

2.17. Let us now assume that expected return is positive (meaning $p < 2/3$), but that our person is not so foolhardy as to stake everything on the risky asset. He chooses a more or less balanced portfolio, that is, a value of a such that $dU/da = 0$:

(3) $-pu'(W - a) + 2(1 - p)u'(W + 2a) = 0.$

This equation expresses implicitly the optimal $a = a^*$ as a function of the exogenous variables W and p; i.e., to any pair (W, p) there corresponds a particular optimal solution:

$$a^* = h(W, p).$$

To illustrate, let us again consider the case with $u(Y) = \ln Y$; the condition is then

$$-\frac{p}{W-a} + \frac{2(1-p)}{W+2a} = 0$$

which gives the solution

$$a^* = h(W, p) = \frac{2 - 3p}{2} W = \frac{\mathcal{E}(X)}{2} W.$$

We see that for this particular preference structure the *proportion* of initial wealth being invested is *constant* (independent of the size of initial wealth); for example, that if $p = 1/2$, the proportion is equal to 25 per cent.

If, on the other hand, we had a quadratic utility function $u(Y) = Y - cY^2$, the condition would have been

$$-p[1 - 2c(W - a)] + 2(1 - p)[1 - 2c(W + 2a)] = 0$$

with the solution

$$a^* = \frac{(1 - 2cW)\mathcal{E}(X)}{2c(4 - 3p)} = \frac{u'(W)\mathcal{E}(X)}{2c(4 - 3p)}.$$

Here we notice that the optimal value a^* *decreases* with wealth. Thus, the greater the wealth, the less should be invested in the risky asset.

2.18. These examples should indicate yet another possibility for tracking down a person's utility function, namely, by studying *the effects of changes in the exogenous variables*. If we find it reasonable that an increase in wealth should lead to an increase in the risky investment, we can at least conclude that the utility function *cannot* be quadratic. But can anything more be concluded on this basis? Or, if we found more specifically that an investor would divide his wealth in fixed proportions at all wealth levels, we know that one utility function which can explain this is the logarithmic. Perhaps others can, too, but which ones?

The fact is that fairly strong restrictions can be placed on the form of the utility function on the basis of simple assumptions about (or observations of) the wealth effect (i.e., the relationship between W and a^*) in such simple decision situations. To see how this can be accomplished, we shall have to return to our discussion of risk aversion.

2.19. We have seen that risk aversion is present if (and only if) $u''(Y) < 0$. It might now be tempting to get a measure of the *strength* of the risk aversion by using values of $u''(Y)$, for example, such that stronger risk aversion went with larger absolute values of $u''(Y)$. But since $u''(Y)$ is determined only up to a constant factor—that is, any multiple of $u''(Y)$ expresses the same preference ordering—the numerical value of $u''(Y)$ is of no consequence; hence, such a measure of risk aversion will not work.

We would like a measure based on $u''(Y)$ however, but which is invariant under linear transformations of the utility function. One such measure would be $u''(Y)/u'(Y)$. To get a positive number we might take the absolute value and call the result,

$$R(Y) = -\frac{u''(Y)}{u'(Y)}$$

the *risk aversion function*. We shall indicate how values of this function do indeed reflect strength of risk aversion.

We have described risk aversion as unwillingness to engage in fair gambles. Now consider a person with wealth W faced with the prospect of winning or losing an amount h with equal probability. Let the certainty equivalent of this prospect be W_0 defined by

(4) $u(W_0) = \tfrac{1}{2}u(W - h) + \tfrac{1}{2}u(W + h).$

Clearly, if the person is risk averse, W_0 is smaller than W, and it would be quite natural to say that his risk aversion is stronger, the larger the difference between W and W_0. This difference,

$$\pi = W - W_0,$$

is sometimes called a *risk premium;* the larger its value, the larger the compensation needed to offset the loss of utility from accepting the uncertain prospect. Substituting for W_0 in (4), we have

(5) $u(W - \pi) = \tfrac{1}{2}u(W - h) + \tfrac{1}{2}u(W + h).$

The first-order approximation to the left-hand side (LHS) is $U(W) - \pi U'(W)$, while the second-order approximation to the right-hand side (RHS) is $U(W) + \tfrac{1}{2}h^2 U''(W)$. Normally, π will be quite small compared to h;[5] hence, the two approximations should represent roughly the same degree of accuracy. Substituting, we then have

$$U(W) - \pi u'(W) \simeq U(W) + \tfrac{1}{2}h^2 u''(W)$$

giving

$$\pi \simeq \tfrac{1}{2}h^2 \left[-\frac{u''(W)}{u'(W)} \right].$$

[5]For example, the author feels that for $h = \$100$, π should be of the order of magnitude of $\$10$.

or

(6) $$\pi \simeq \tfrac{1}{2}h^2 R(W).$$

Thus, to the extent that the approximations are valid, the risk premium increases proportionally with the value of the risk aversion function. This result was first presented by Pratt [6].

2.20. The relation (6) is offered principally as an *interpretation* of the risk aversion function. As such it is clearly useful, but, because of its approximate nature, its importance should not be exaggerated. Actually, we are not so much interested in the numerical value of the risk premium as in how it would change with changes in the wealth level. Other things equal, would we expect a rich man to require a larger or a smaller compensation than someone less well-to-do for engaging in a given risky prospect? In other words, what do we expect about the sign of $d\pi/dW$?

By implicit differentiation of (5) we obtain

$$\frac{d\pi}{dW} = \frac{u'(W - \pi) - \tfrac{1}{2}u'(W - h) - \tfrac{1}{2}u'(W + h)}{u'(W - \pi)}$$

Since u' is positive, the effect will be of the same sign as the numerator

$$N(h) = u'(W - \pi) - \tfrac{1}{2}u'(W - h) - \tfrac{1}{2}u'(W + h).$$

Clearly, $N(0) = 0$, since $h = 0$ implies $\pi = 0$. Therefore, if we can determine the sign of $N'(h)$ we shall also know the sign of N. Differentiation gives

$$N'(h) = -u''(W - \pi)\frac{d\pi}{dh} + \frac{1}{2}u''(W - h) - \frac{1}{2}u''(W + h).$$

By differentiating (5) we obtain

$$\frac{d\pi}{dh} = \frac{\tfrac{1}{2}u'(W - h) - \tfrac{1}{2}u'(W + h)}{u'(W - \pi)},$$

hence

$$N'(h) = \frac{1}{2}u''(W - h) - \frac{1}{2}u''(W + h)$$
$$- \frac{u''(W - \pi)}{u'(W - \pi)}\left[\frac{1}{2}u'(W - h) - \frac{1}{2}u'(W + h)\right]$$
$$= \left[\frac{1}{2}u'(W - h) - \frac{1}{2}u'(W + h)\right]$$
$$\times \left[\frac{u''(W - h) - u''(W + h)}{u'(W - h) - u'(W + h)} + R(W - \pi)\right].$$

With $u'' < 0$, the first term is clearly positive, so that the sign of $N'(h)$ is the same as that of the second term.

First suppose $R(Y)$ is decreasing. Since $\pi < h$, we have $W - h < W - \pi$; hence $R(W - h) > R(W - \pi)$, or

$$-\frac{u''(W - h)}{u'(W - h)} > R(W - \pi),$$

in other words,

(7) $$u''(W - h) < -R(W - \pi)u'(W - h).$$

Trivially, $W + h > W - \pi$, so that in the same way we have

(8) $$-u''(W + h) < R(W - \pi)u'(W + h).$$

Adding the inequalities (7) and (8) yields

$$u''(W - h) - u''(W + h) < -R(W - \pi)[u'(W - h) - u'(W + h)],$$

implying that the second term in the expression for $N'(h)$ is uniformly negative. This in turn implies that $N(h)$ is uniformly negative, which in turn implies that $d\pi/dW$ is negative. Obviously, if $R(Y)$ is increasing, the effect is reversed. We have thus established an important relationship between the wealth effect on the risk premium and the slope of the risk aversion function: A risk premium decreasing with wealth is compatible only with a decreasing risk aversion function, and vice versa.

2.21. Whether the risk premium does or does not decrease with the wealth level is of course an empirical question. On intuitive grounds, or from casual observation, most people would probably find a decrease as the most natural hypothesis. Let us therefore examine the implications of such an hypothesis for the wealth effect in our portfolio problem.

If we differentiate implicitly in (3) with respect to W, we obtain

$$\frac{da}{dW} = -\frac{1}{D}[-pu''(W - a) + 2(1 - p)u''(W + 2a)],$$

where $D = d^2U/da^2 < 0$, so that the effect is of the same sign as the expression in brackets. If $R(Y)$ is now decreasing we have $R(W - a) > R(W)$, or

$$-\frac{u''(W - a)}{u'(W - a)} > R(W)$$

and so

(9) $$-pu''(W - a) > pR(W)u'(W - a).$$

In the same way we have $R(W + 2a) < R(W)$, or

$$-\frac{u''(W + 2a)}{u'(W + 2a)} < R(W),$$

so that

(10) $2(1 - p)u''(W + 2a) > -2(1 - p)R(W)u'(W + 2a).$

Adding (9) and (10) therefore gives

$$-pu''(W - a) + 2(1 - p)u''(W + 2a)$$
$$> -R(W)[-pu'(W - a) + 2(1 - p)u'(W + 2a)].$$

But from the first-order condition (3) for a maximum we know that the expression in brackets on the RHS is zero. Hence the LHS is positive, and so $da/dW > 0$.

For the two examples given above we find $R(Y)$ as:

$u(Y) = \ln Y;$ $R(Y) = 1/Y$, i.e., decreasing;

$u(Y) = Y - cY^2;$ $R(Y) = \dfrac{2c}{1 - 2cY}$, i.e., increasing.

This and other properties of a quadratic utility function will be discussed further below.

2.22.   Before drawing conclusions which are too far-reaching on the basis of our simple portfolio example, we shall briefly examine a decision problem from a different field. Consider a person about to buy fire insurance on his house. The elements of the problem are the following: The value of the house is L, and in addition he owns other wealth in the amount W. The damage which may occur is a stochastic variable X with probability distribution

x	$g(x)$
L	p
0	$1 - p$

that is, the house will either be completely destroyed with probability p, or will suffer no damage at all. Expected damage is thus $\mathcal{E}(X) = pL$.

If our person buys full coverage, the premium will be P. However, nothing but the insistence of the insurance agent can prevent him from underinsuring, and we shall assume that he is interested in determining an optimal *coverage ratio*, k. With coverage k the premium he pays will be only

kP, while the compensation from the company will be only kX when the damage is X. The outcome of his decision, final wealth, is thus a stochastic variable of the form

$$Y = W + L - kP - X + kX$$

with the distribution

y	$f(y)$
$W + kL - kP$	p
$W + L - kP$	$1 - p$

Expected utility under such an arrangement is therefore

$$U = pu(W + kL - kP) + (1 - p)u(W + L - kP)$$

and the problem is to find the value of k ($0 \leq k \leq 1$) that maximizes expected utility.

From this model the reader can easily verify that the condition for taking full coverage (choosing $k = 1$) is that

$$P \leq \mathcal{E}(X).$$

This is the same as requiring the gross premium to be smaller than the expected damage, i.e., the premium must be actuarially unfavorable for the company. Since such premiums have never been heard of, we must conclude that a rational person will never take full coverage. This result is completely analogous to our conclusion from the portfolio problem: If expected "return" from taking risk is positive, *some* risk taking will always be profitable.

In this problem it is also fairly straightforward to derive the wealth effect on the willingness to provide insurance coverage, i.e., dk/dW. Following the same general procedure as before, we will find that the effect is negative if $R(Y)$ is decreasing. This result is also analogous to our conclusion from the portfolio problem: The richer you are, the more risk you carry yourself.

2.23. Without going into the details, it may be mentioned that conclusions of the same general nature can be drawn from assumptions about another measure of risk aversion, the function $-u''(Y)Y/u'(Y)$, which is referred to as *relative* (as opposed to R as *absolute*) risk aversion. For example, it can be shown that if the *proportion* held of the risky asset decreases with the size of the portfolio, then relative risk aversion is an increasing function of wealth (see [1]).

The remarkable thing about these results is that assumptions about behavior in simple decision situations, which we may easily observe in real life, can place fairly strong restrictions on the utility function. I believe that an important research task in the area of decision theory or the "economics of uncertainty" lies precisely in this type of analysis: using observations of behavior, or "reasonable" assumptions about rational behavior in different circumstances, to isolate the class of utility functions which can represent this behavior.

This task has been aptly formulated by Pratt [6], and I should like to quote a passage from his article because it expresses so nicely the right way of *viewing* the problems in decision theory. After having discussed the relationships between assumptions about the two risk aversion functions and the wealth effect in insurance and portfolio problems, he says:

> These results have both descriptive and normative implications. Utility functions for which [absolute risk aversion] is decreasing are logical candidates to use when trying to describe the behavior of people who, one feels, might generally pay less for insurance against a given risk the greater their assets. And consideration of the yield and riskiness per investment dollar of investor's portfolios may suggest, at least in some contexts, descriptions by utility functions for which [relative risk aversion] is first decreasing and then increasing.
>
> Normatively, it seems likely that many decision makers would feel they ought to pay less for insurance against a given risk the greater their assets. Such a decision maker will want to choose a utility function for which [absolute risk aversion] is decreasing, adding this condition to the others he must already consider (consistency and probably concavity) in forging a satisfactory utility from more or less malleable preliminary preferences. He may wish to add a further condition on [relative risk aversion].[6]

The common conclusion for both the portfolio problem and the insurance problem was that if an individual has decreasing risk aversion, he will assume more risk the larger his wealth. On the face of it, such a statement may look like a tautology: "If your risk aversion decreases with your wealth, then the amount of risk you assume increases with your wealth." However, the assumption is one concerning the individual's (unobservable) structure of preferences over probability distributions, while the *conclusion* concerns his (observable) behavior under various conditions. That is, the assumption of decreasing risk aversion serves as a tool for advancing meaningful hypotheses about actual behavior. If anything, the resemblance to a tautology merely reflects the fact that the name "risk aversion function" given to the function $-u''(Y)/u'(Y)$ is particularly well chosen in view of its behavioral implications.

2.24.   We have seen that a quadratic utility function exhibits increasing risk aversion. Casual empirical observation would therefore seem to rule out such a utility function as very useful for explaining or predicting

---

[6]J. Pratt, "Risk Aversion in the Small and in the Large," *Econometrica*, 1965, pp. 122–123.

actual behavior. Nevertheless, the use—often implicit—of such a utility function has a long tradition in the analysis of decisions under uncertainty, and we shall also find it useful throughout this book because of its mathematical simplicity and sometimes intuitive appeal. The expectation of a quadratic function is expressed in terms of the mean and the variance of the variable only, and these terms are familiar to anyone with a cursory knowledge of statistics. However, careless use of a quadratic utility function may lead to questionable or even paradoxical conclusions, and it is only fair to note briefly some of the problems involved.

Concern with quadratic utility functions is clearly closely related to the mean-standard deviation approach to decision making, an approach that in principle assumes that all relevant information about a probability distribution is contained in its first two moments. The first point to be made is that if the probability distributions under consideration are all completely described by two parameters (as, e.g., the normal distribution), then there is nothing wrong with such a procedure. In many practical situations this assumption may seem reasonable, but there are important classes of probability distributions which are not fully determined by just two parameters. Consider, for example, the choice between the following two-point distributions:

y	$f_1(y)$	y	$f_2(y)$
2	1/4	4	3/4
6	3/4	8	1/4

A reader accustomed to thinking in terms of mean and standard deviation (or variance) only is urged to make a serious mental effort to compare two distributions such as these. Computation shows that both distributions have means of 5 and variances of 3, but is there really any convincing reason why they may not be ranked differently?

2.25. It was asserted earlier that if a person consistently (i.e., for any set of probability distributions) uses a mean-standard deviation criterion, his behavior can only be represented by means of a quadratic utility function. To some people this proposition apparently seems perfectly obvious, to others much less so. For the benefit of the latter group we shall discuss it in somewhat more detail.

The choices of such a person is often analyzed by means of an indifference map in the E, S plane where an indifference curve represents all E, S combinations that are considered equally good. Suppose our person tells us that he is indifferent between the probability distributions $f_1(y)$ and $f_2(y)$ which have means E_1, E_2 and standard deviations S_1, S_2, respectively. By our rationality assumptions, he should not mind letting chance decide which one he gets, so we let him have f_1 with probability p and f_2 with probability $1 - p$. Under this procedure he is faced with the distribution

$$f(y) = pf_1(y) + (1 - p)f_2(y)$$

which has mean and variance

$$E = pE_1 + (1 - p)E_2$$
$$S^2 = pS_1^2 + (1 - p)S_2^2 + p(1 - p)(E_1 - E_2)^2.$$

Any such E, S combination must therefore lie on the same indifference curve as (E_1, S_1) and (E_2, S_2). By eliminating p between the two expressions, we obtain, after some manipulation, a relationship between E and S of the form

(11) $E - c(E^2 + S^2) = \text{constant},$

where c is a parameter determined by the location of the points (E_1, S_1) and (E_2, S_2). This relationship defines the indifference curve between (E_1, S_1) and (E_2, S_2). Since an indifference curve is nothing but the locus of points with constant expected utility, we have

$$\mathcal{E}[u(Y)] = E - c(E^2 + S^2),$$

which obviously implies $U(Y) = Y - cY^2$.

We also note that (11) can alternatively be written as

$$S^2 + (E - k)^2 = \text{constant},$$

which represents a circle with center on the E axis. If this procedure is repeated for all other points between which our person is indifferent, and if certain simple continuity conditions hold, it is clear that all indifference curves must be concentric circles with center on the E axis. The implications of an E, S criterion are therefore rather strong and should cause more concern than we usually find in discussions of decision making based on this criterion.

2.26.   Suppose we present our person with the following problem. He may choose between a probability distribution with a mean of 100 and a standard deviation of 30, and one with an undetermined mean x and a standard deviation of 40. We then ask him which value of x would make him indifferent between the two. Being a risk averter, he will certainly require an x larger than 100; suppose his answer is $x = 110$. We then ask him to consider the following two distributions:

y	$f_1(y)$	y	$f_2(y)$
70	1/2	70	1/2
130	1/2	150	1/2

He would certainly have to be considered very stupid if he did not prefer f_2. So we finally ask him to compute the means and the standard deviations for the two distributions. To his (but probably not the reader's) astonishment, he finds

$$E_1 = 100, \quad S_1 = 30$$
$$E_2 = 110, \quad S_2 = 40.$$

The explanation of this and similar paradoxes is not far to seek. After a point, a quadratic utility function will start to fall, and rigid adherence to such a utility function will lead to nonsense decisions. A utility function $u(Y) = Y - cY^2$ will reach its maximum at $Y = 1/2c$, so values of Y above this level will be given increasingly smaller weights. The reader should be able to verify that indifference between the distributions (100, 30) and (110, 40) implies that $1/2c = 140$. This explains why 130 and 150 are given the same weight, and therefore why the two distributions above would be ranked indifferently by the E, S criterion.

In addition to these problems, we have already noted that a quadratic utility function also has the disconcerting property of increasing risk aversion. This property is of an entirely different nature, however. Even restricting attention to values of Y for which $u(Y)$ is increasing, we cannot avoid increasing $R(Y)$ and the questionable conclusions to which this leads. Increasing $R(Y)$ is a global property of this particular utility function, i.e., it holds for any value of Y.

2.27. The various problems associated with the use of a quadratic utility function (or an E, S criterion) should be kept in mind, but it may still be argued that a quadratic utility function serves a useful purpose as a simple approximation to any given utility function over a specified set of values of outcomes. Considered as such, the value of c should clearly be changed if the range of possible outcomes is changed. Thus, an increase in initial wealth would normally imply an upward shift in the range of outcomes; and approximation by a quadratic would then require a decrease in c. Looking back at the expression for the optimal solution for the portfolio problem, we see that the result may indeed be the more plausible one of an increase in a.

2.28. In the formulation of our hypotheses, two critical elements appear: the slope of the risk aversion function and the level of initial wealth. This immediately raises two important questions. First, on what basis are we entitled to make assumptions about the shape of the risk aversion function? Second, how is initial wealth to be measured? Both of these problems are usually neglected in the literature on theories of risk taking based on the expected utility approach. To warn against overly simple-minded interpretations of the theory, these problems should be briefly discussed (even if not resolved).

2.29. The problem of specification of the utility function in terms of which alternative decisions are evaluated is principally of a theoretical nature. When a utility function u of final wealth Y is postulated, the assumption is implicit that Y can be considered as representing future consumption opportunities. It is therefore clear that u must somehow reflect preferences with respect to ultimate consumption variables. This relationship may be clarified by considering the following simple situation: A person is to make a decision now which will bring his wealth to a (random) level Y. When a value y of this variable materializes, he plans to spend it all on the consumption of two goods whose prices he knows will be 1 and p; after this, nothing else matters. Denote the amounts consumed by x_1 and x_2, and let us assume that our person, by the procedure of comparing gambles among commodity bundles, has managed to express his preferences by a cardinal utility function $f(x_1, x_2)$, say $f(x_1, x_2) = \ln x_1 x_2$. The optimal decision will therefore be $x_1 = y/2$, $x_2 = y/2p$, with the resulting maximum utility level

$$\max_{x_1, x_2} f(x_1, x_2) = \ln(y^2/4p),$$

which is equivalent, as a utility function, to $\ln y$. Thus, in this case, the relevant utility function for evaluation of the *immediate* decision is $u(Y) = \ln Y$. This is referred to as the "derived" or "indirect" utility function (relative to the subsequent consumption opportunities).

It is clear that if the immediate decision is the only one that will affect Y, then $\mathcal{E}[u(Y)]$ is the appropriate evaluator of that decision. However, when the present decision constitutes but one in a sequence of decisions to be taken before the target date of wealth accumulation, it can be evaluated in terms of u only on a second level of indirectness as part of a complete optimal strategy for subsequent decisions. In that case the function ϕ, whose expectation is to be maximized by the immediate decision, is the *maximum* of $\mathcal{E}[u(Y)]$ with respect to all subsequent decisions. Without specifying details of the complete sequence of decision problems, little can be said in general about the relationship between u and ϕ. This means that even if it were known that u exhibits decreasing risk aversion, it is not necessarily true that ϕ also does so. For a discussion of some of these aspects, see [5]. The situation is further complicated when there is not a single consumption target but a whole sequence of consumption decisions to be made. We cannot take up these problems in detail, but refer the reader to Fama [2].

2.30. One problem raised by the analysis of decisions with repercussions into the future should be pointed out. The difficulty is caused by the difference between a *temporal* and *timeless* prospect.

Consider the following two situations. In both situations I offer you $1000 if a coin comes up heads, and in both situations the amount will be payable one year from today. However, in one situation the coin is tossed today (a timeless prospect), in the other a year from today (a temporal prospect). In both situations we are concerned with a probability distribution

x	$f(x)$
0	1/2
1000	1/2

but you would obviously prefer to have the coin tossed today so that you know what your position is and can plan accordingly. So it is clear that the temporal aspect will affect your choice. More important than that, however, is the fact that it may not even be possible to represent such choices by means of a utility function. We know that if this is so, the rule for making the choices violates our rationality conditions. We shall examine this problem in the context of a simple two-period consumption model.

Consider an individual faced with the problem of allocating his wealth Y between present consumption c_1 and future consumption c_2. To make things simple we assume that the interest rate on savings (positive or negative) is zero with certainty. Thus, $c_2 = Y - c_1$. Total wealth could be conceived of as consisting of present income Y_1 and future income Y_2, with Y_1 known and Y_2 being a random variable. It is only their sum that matters, however; the crucial point is that the precise value of Y will not become known before the end of the initial period, i.e., after c_1 has been chosen. The probability distribution for Y, $f(y)$, thus represents a temporal prospect.

Determination of an optimal value of c_1 requires the existence of a cardinal utility function $u(c_1, c_2)$ representing preferences among consumption profiles (or rather among probability distributions for consumption profiles). This function satisfies our rationality assumptions. Thus, when the optimal c_1 is chosen, expected utility is

$$U(f) = \max_{c_1} \mathcal{E}[u(c_1, Y - c_1)].$$

This expression defines indirectly the preference index associated with the probability distribution $f(y)$ and thus establishes a preference ordering over all such distributions. The question now is: Can this preference ordering be represented by means of a utility function $v(Y)$ for wealth? That is, is it possible to write

$$\max_{c_1} \mathcal{E}[u(c_1, Y - c_1)] = \mathcal{E}[v(Y)]?$$

It is easy to demonstrate that such a representation does not generally exist.

To see what is involved, consider an example with the utility function

$$u(c_1, c_2) = 200 - (10 - c_1)^2 - (10 - c_2)^2 \qquad (c_1 < 10, c_2 < 10)$$

Substituting $c_2 = Y - c_1$, this becomes

$$u(c_1, Y - c_1) = 200 - (10 - c_1)^2 - (10 + c_1)^2 + 2(10 + c_1)Y - Y^2,$$

so that expected utility is

$$\mathcal{E}[u(c_1, Y - c_1)]$$
$$= 200 - (10 - c_1)^2 - (10 + c_1)^2 + 2(10 + c_1)E - E^2 - S^2,$$

where E and S are the mean and standard deviation of Y. The optimal value of c_1 is here given by $c_1 = E/2$, which, upon substitution, gives the preference index

$$U(f) = \max_{c_1} \mathcal{E}[u(c_1, Y - c_1)] = 200 - \tfrac{1}{2}(20 - E)^2 - S^2.$$

This formula could be used to plot indifference curves for such prospects in the E, S plane; these would be ellipses with center at (20, 0) and eccentricity 1/2. But we know that for an arbitrary probability distribution no function $v(Y)$ makes such a representation possible; the only utility function giving expected utility in terms of E and S only is the quadratic, and in that case the indifference curves are circles.

     The explanation of this result is not far to seek. Consider a specific distribution $f_1(y)$ such that $Y = 9$ or $Y = 17$ with equal probability. This has mean $E_1 = 13$ and standard deviation $S_1 = 4$. Under this prospect the preference index is $U(f_1) = 159.5$. This distribution has the same preference index as the *certain* outcome $Y = 11$, or, to put it differently, the individual is indifferent between $f_1(y)$ and the degenerate distribution $f_2(y)$ which gives $Y = 11$ with certainty. He may then consider letting the choice be decided by a coin toss. This device may seem simple enough, but in a temporal context it must be used with care—it makes a great deal of difference whether the coin is tossed now or a year from now. If the coin is tossed *now* everything is fine. He will know which of the two distributions will apply, and in either case he will, by choosing the appropriate c_1, obtain a utility level of 159.5, hence he should not mind letting chance decide which one will apply.

     If the coin is to be tossed *after* c_1 has been chosen, however, he faces the temporal prospect $f(y) = \tfrac{1}{2}f_1(y) + \tfrac{1}{2}f_2(y)$:

y	$f(y)$
9	1/4
11	1/2
17	1/4

For this prospect, $E = 12$ and $S = 3$, so that the corresponding preference index would be $U(f) = 159$. Thus, the distribution f ranks below f_1 and f_2, i.e., $U(\frac{1}{2}f_1 + \frac{1}{2}f_2) < U(f_1)$ even though $U(f_1) = U(f_2)$. This represents an obvious violation of our rationality conditions for an expected utility representation of $U(f)$. Such a representation requires that $U(\alpha f_1 + (1 - \alpha)f_2) = \alpha U(f_1) + (1 - \alpha)U(f_2)$ for any two distributions.

It is not difficult to see why this condition is not satisfied. In determining his optimal c_1 under the mixed prospect f, the individual will take into account the need for hedging against the uncertain outcome of the coin toss. But a decision made on this basis is quite obviously optimal against *neither* of the original distributions f_1 or f_2. Relative to f_1 he will, in retrospect, have consumed too little; relative to f_2, too much. The example demonstrates the importance of the temporal aspect in risk-taking situations. The representation of preferences among probability distributions by means of a utility function of wealth is meant to apply to cases of timeless prospects, i.e., to situations in which the outcome is determined at once, without any intervening decisions involving commitment of the outcome. For such prospects, derivation of an indirect utility function for wealth from the solution of the allocation problem causes no difficulty. For temporal prospects, however, representation of preferences in terms of a utility function for wealth may be inappropriate—and for reasons that are obvious once they are realized. What is more, in the real world *temporal* prospects, not timeless ones, are the rule rather than the exception; the holding of a portfolio of securities is a typical example. In spite of this problem, we shall have to proceed, crossing our fingers, on the assumption that investors' behavior satisfies our rationality conditions, making possible a representation of preferences in terms of expected utility of wealth. In spite of all theoretical difficulties, it is of course possible (and meaningful) to test behavioral hypotheses like those we have advanced.

2.31. The second problem mentioned above concerns the appropriate definition, or measure, of "initial wealth." This question is more immediately relevant for purposes of empirical testing, although it is closely related to the problem of specification of the utility function.

Again the issue may be clarified by reference to some simplified situations. In the case of a single subsequent consumption target examined above, Y represented the (random) amount available for consumption and must therefore be identified with the value of the individual's *marketable assets* as of the time of consumption. Since Y is simply W plus the net outcome of the immediate decision, W must correspondingly be taken as the current value of marketable assets. That is, W is the amount that could be obtained by liquidating all assets in order to spend the proceeds on consumption.

Faced with a more complex future, the appropriate measure of W may be different, however. Consider next the following situation: The immediate decision will bring the value of marketable assets to the random amount Y. When a value y of this variate is realized, the individual will with certainty receive annual incomes v_i for the rest of his life (the length n of which is also taken as known), and he will decide upon annual amounts of consumption c_i in order to maximize some preference ordering $f(c_1, \ldots, c_n)$. It is further assumed that a constant, known interest rate will prevail throughout his lifetime. Under these conditions we can meaningfully measure the present value of future incomes as $v = \sum \beta^i v_i$ (where β is the discount factor), and therefore also the individuals's net worth, z, as the sum of marketable assets and present value of future incomes: $z = y + v$. The budget restraint is of the form $\sum \beta^i c_i = z$, and it is clear that the maximum utility level is determined uniquely by z: $\max f(c_1, \ldots, c_n) = \phi(z)$. Therefore, the appropriate measure of initial wealth in this case should include the present value of future incomes.

Consider, however, what happens if the assumption of certain future incomes and interest rate is dropped; these are now random variables described in terms of some joint probability distribution. Then it is only possible for the individual to adopt an optimal (contingent) consumption *strategy* and to calculate the corresponding expected maximum utility level (conditional upon the strategy being optimal). But this maximum of expected utility can evidently be expressed only in terms of y and parameters θ of the probability distribution for incomes and interest rate, say as $\phi(y; \theta)$, which as before is the relevant utility function for evaluating the immediate decision. There is no reason why it should be possible to construct an index of the parameters θ that could be compared to v and added to y as above. In this case we are led to consider y as the argument of a derived utility function $\psi(y)$, with everything else about the future being absorbed in the form of this function. We are therefore back to marketable assets as the measure of initial wealth. To illustrate: It is to be expected that a man who has just completed his Ph.D. will behave differently from an unskilled laborer, even if they each own identical amounts of marketable assets and have identical preference structures over future consumption possibilities. This need not be interpreted as an indication that the value of marketable assets is a poor measure of initial wealth; the difference is accounted for by the different *derived* utility functions ψ, because these depend upon the probability distributions that each man will encounter, which will generally be quite different.

It is also trivial that even in the case of complete certainty it is possible to consider differences in future incomes as being absorbed in the form of the derived utility function, that is, to write $\phi(y + v_1) = \psi_1(y)$; $\phi(y + v_2) = \psi_2(y)$, and so on, for different values of v.

It may seem like hairsplitting to try to establish whether a change in future incomes "should" be accounted for by the form of the derived utility function or by the value of its argument. It should be kept in mind, however, that the kind of hypotheses we have advanced are *not* concerned with future decision problems but with effect on *immediate* decisions, and for this problem it seems that the measure of W most generally relevant as an argument of the utility function is the value of the individual's marketable assets.

Even if this may be correct on the theoretical level, not all problems connected with empirical testing are thus resolved. But this is due to the well-known incongruity between the nature of the hypothesis to be tested and the nature of the available data. The hypothesis concerns a single individual's decisions under alternative, hypothetical, levels of initial wealth, while the data typically consists of observations on different individuals' actual decisions. These individuals differ with respect to basic consumption preferences, marketable assets, and the kind of future they face. The first type of difference is unobservable and of the type which we hope will cancel out in the sample of observations, thus enabling us to evaluate the effect of the other differences. Now suppose we choose to measure initial wealth by the value of marketable assets. If marketable assets were uncorrelated with the kind of future individuals face, we might even hope that these differences would cancel out in the sample. But they are not uncorrelated, and for that reason the relationship between risk bearing and marketable assets as evidenced by the sample observations may contain spurious correlations (the form of the derived utility functions and their arguments being systematically related to each other). It is easy to think of situations that may cause both of the classical error types: rejecting the hypothesis when it is in fact true, and accepting it when it is in fact false. We shall not pursue this, but would think that the most important of such errors might be accounted for by differences in *age* and *education* (compare the example given earlier).

How this should be handled statistically is largely a technical question. One might just subdivide the sample by age and educational level and study each subgroup independently, or one might prefer to work directly with a model with three independent variables. A more tempting possibility would be to construct a single index of all three, and it would be difficult not to think of this as some measure of net worth. This may be a perfectly acceptable procedure as long as we realize that when institutional arrangements are such that certainty equivalents for future random patterns of income and interest rates are not traded in the market, any such measure is in general only a proxy variable. When the future is uncertain, there is in principle no meaningful measure of expected present value of future incomes which can enter as an argument of a utility function. It is probably not generally meaningful to speak of present value of future incomes as a scalar stochastic variable; even if it were, and its expectation could be calculated, it would not be relevant as part of the argument of the utility function. This can be made clear by considering an individual who, after making an immediate decision which will bring his marketable assets to Y, will receive an additional random amount V (independent of the immediate decision), and who then will make a single consumption decision. The relevant evaluator of the immediate decision is $\mathcal{E}[U(Y + V)]$, which is (in general) quite a different thing from $\mathcal{E}\{U[Y + \mathcal{E}(V)]\}$.

As an approximation, however, some measure of net worth based on future income potential might perform excellently for predicting behavior on both the individual and the aggregate level. And, after all, the ultimate criterion of the usefulness of a specified measure of initial wealth is its ability to produce good predictions.

REFERENCES

1. Arrow, K. J. *Aspects of the Theory of Risk-Bearing.* Helsinki: The Yrjö Jahnsson Foundation, 1965.
2. Fama, E. F. "Multiperiod Consumption—Investment Decisions," *Amer. Econ. Rev.*, 1970, pp. 163–174.
3. Friedman, M., and L. J. Savage. "The Utility Analysis of Choices Involving Risk," *Jour. Pol. Econ.*, 1948, pp. 279–304.
4. Knight, F. H. *Risk, Uncertainty, and Profit.* New York: Houghton Mifflin & Co., 1921.
5. Mossin, J. "Optimal Multiperiod Portfolio Policies," *Jour. Bus.*, 1968, pp. 215–229.
6. Pratt, J. "Risk Aversion in the Small and in the Large," *Econometrica*, 1964, pp. 122–136.
7. Savage, L. J. *Foundations of Statistics.* New York: John Wiley & Sons, 1952.

3 Portfolio Theory:

The Demand for Securities

3.1. The purpose of this chapter is to describe an investor's demand for the various securities available in the market. This means that we want to specify the functional relationships between the quantities he wishes to buy of the various securities and the prices and return characteristics of those securities. In the previous chapter we examined an extremely simple version of such a portfolio selection problem; in this chapter we shall generalize and extend that analysis and relate it to the existing literature. The generalization will proceed in several steps.

3.2. Our first step is to allow an arbitrary probability distribution for the return on the risky asset—not necessarily a two-point distribution. Otherwise the model and the notation are precisely the same: two assets, one of which is riskless with a zero interest. We shall denote the random return, which has the dimension of an interest rate, by X, and write its distribution as $f(x)$. The two components of final wealth are the value of the riskless investment, $W - a$, and the end value of the risky investment, $a(1 + X)$. Thus,

$$Y = W + aX.$$

As before, the preferred portfolio is the one which maximizes

(1)
$$U = \mathcal{E}[u(Y)] = \sum_x u(W + ax)f(x).$$

The first two derivatives with respect to a are

$$\frac{dU}{da} = \mathcal{E}[u'(Y)X] = \sum_x u'(W + ax)xf(x)$$

$$\frac{d^2U}{da^2} = \mathcal{E}[u''(Y)X^2] = \sum_x u''(W + ax)x^2f(x).$$

With $u'' < 0$, the second derivative is again negative. If the first derivative is evaluated at $a = 0$, we obtain as before

$$\left.\frac{dU}{da}\right|_{a=0} = u'(W)\mathcal{E}(X),$$

so that the conclusion that $a = 0$ if and only if $\mathcal{E}(X) \le 0$ carries over to the more general case.

If an interior value of a is selected, we have at this point

(2)
$$\mathcal{E}[u'(Y)X] = 0.$$

This condition can be interpreted in the following way: Since X is the (random) return per dollar invested in the risky asset, $u'(Y)X$ is the random utility increment from investing an additional dollar; investment is thus carried out to the point where the expected utility increment becomes zero.

It is also in this case straightforward to relate the wealth effect to the slope of the risk aversion function. By implicit differentiation of (2) we obtain

$$\frac{da}{dW} = -\frac{\mathcal{E}[u''(Y)X]}{\mathcal{E}[u''(Y)X^2]},$$

so that the sign is the same as $\mathcal{E}[u''(Y)X]$. Assume now that $R(Y)$ is decreasing, and consider first the case when $X < 0$. This means that $Y < W$ and hence $R(Y) > R(W)$, or

(3)
$$-\frac{u''(Y)}{u'(Y)} > R(W).$$

X being negative, multiplication by $-u'(Y)X$ does not change the inequality; hence

(4)
$$u''(Y)X > -R(W)u'(Y)X.$$

Now consider the case when $X > 0$, implying $Y > W$. Then the inequality (3) is reversed, but multiplication by $-u'(Y)X$ now reverses it once more, so that (4) holds for all values of X. Taking expectations in (4) gives

$$\mathcal{E}[u''(Y)X] > -R(W)\mathcal{E}[u'(Y)X] = 0,$$

since $R(W)$ is not a random variable. Consequently $da/dW > 0$. If we require $da/dW > 0$ for any W and arbitrary probability distributions, a monotonically decreasing $R(Y)$ also becomes a necessary condition.[1]

3.3.   Let us again consider the application of (2) to a quadratic utility function. We have here

$$u'(Y) = 1 - 2cY = (1 - 2cW) - 2caX,$$

so that (2) becomes

$$\mathcal{E}[(1 - 2cW)X - 2caX^2] = 0$$

or

$$(1 - 2cW)E - 2ca(E^2 + S^2) = 0$$

with solution

(5) $$a = \frac{E}{E^2 + S^2}(1/2c - W)$$

where E and S are the mean and standard deviation of X. Thus, as already noted, both the amount invested as well as the fraction a/W of total wealth depend on W.

As an example, suppose $c = 1/1000$, $W = \$200$, and that the distribution of X is

x	$f(x)$
-1	1/2
2	1/2

so that $E = 1/2$, $E^2 + S^2 = 5/2$. Then the optimal a is \$60.

3.4.   The reader acquainted with the literature on portfolio theory will recognize certain differences between our formulation of the portfolio selection problem and the traditional formulations as represented, e.g., by Tobin [11] or Markowitz [6]. One of the differences consists in the different specification of the outcome of the decision, and also the decision variable

[1] The preceding analysis parallels closely that of Arrow [1].

itself. In our formulation the outcome is described by the dollar amount of final wealth, Y, and the decision variable as the dollar amount invested in the risky asset, a. In the formulations referred to, however, the outcome is described in terms of the *rate of return*, R, on total wealth, while the decision variable is taken as the *fraction*, k, of initial wealth invested in the risky asset. In our terms, R and k would be defined by

$$R = \frac{Y - W}{W}$$

$$k = \frac{a}{W}$$

so that

$$R = \frac{W + aX - W}{W} = \frac{a}{W} X = kX.$$

If a quadratic utility function in rate of return is now postulated, say,

$$v(R) = R - bR^2,$$

expected utility is

$$V = \mathcal{E}[v(R)] = \mathcal{E}[kX - bk^2 X^2] = kE - bk^2(E^2 + S^2)$$

An interior maximum of V then occurs at

(6) $$k = \frac{E}{2b(E^2 + S^2)}.$$

The important point to be made here is that the way (6) is written makes it seem as if the optimal k is independent of initial wealth. In the formulation of the problem, the level of initial wealth has somehow slipped out the back door. In addition, the resulting maximum level of expected utility would seem to be independent of the wealth level.

So it appears to be a conflict between the two formulations. However, a little reflection shows that when initial wealth is taken as a given, constant datum (say, 100), any level of final wealth can obviously be equivalently described either in absolute terms (say, 120) or as a rate of return (.2). What we argue here is that it is immaterial to the investor whether a final wealth level of 120 is a result of an initial wealth level of 80 with a rate of return of .5 or an initial wealth of 100 with a return of .2 [or any other combination of W and R such that $W(1 + R) = 120$]. The explanation of the apparent conflict is now very simple: When using a quadratic utility function in R, the coefficient b is not independent of W if the function shall lead to consistent decisions at different levels of wealth. This is seen by inserting $R = (Y - W)$ $/W$ in $v(R)$; the result is

$$v(R) = \frac{1 + 2b}{W} Y - \frac{b}{W^2} Y^2 - (b + 1),$$

which is equivalent, as a utility function, to

$$Y - \frac{b}{W(1 + 2b)} Y^2.$$

What this implies is that a utility function of the form $R - bR^2$ cannot be used with the same b at different levels of initial wealth. The appropriate value must be set such that $b/W(1 + 2b) = c$, i.e., $b = cW/(1 - 2cW)$. But when this precaution is taken, it is easily verified that the traditional formulation will lead to the correct decision. For example, if the utility function for final wealth is $Y - Y^2/400$, it may be perfectly acceptable to maximize the expectation of $R - R^2/2$, but *only* if initial wealth happens to be 100.

3.5. If attention is not restricted to quadratic utility functions, it may be possible to get investment in the risky asset strictly proportional to initial wealth. We have already seen, in Chapter II, that this will be the case if the utility function is logarithmic. It can be shown that the only other utility functions with this property are the power functions $u(Y) = Y^a$ (a formal proof is given in [7]). Clearly, $\ln Y$ and Y^a are equivalent, as utility functions, to $\ln (1 + R)$ and $(1 + R)^a$, respectively, since they represent linear transformations of each other. The conclusion is therefore that there may exist preferences which can be represented by a utility function in the rate of return only, but it must then be of the form $\ln (1 + R)$ or $(1 + R)^a$. Other forms, like the quadratic with constant b, are ruled out.

3.6. The logarithmic utility function has another interesting property which was first studied by Breiman [2] and further developed by Hakansson [5]. Suppose the immediate portfolio decision constitutes but one in a sequence of portfolio decisions to be made in the future. That is, we consider the investor as starting out with a given wealth level W and making a first-period decision on the allocation of this wealth to different assets, then waiting until the end of the period when a new wealth level Y materializes, then making a second-period decision on the allocation of Y, and so forth. Consider now the following alternative formulations of objectives for his portfolio policy:

1. The policy should be such that a given target wealth level is reached in the shortest possible expected time;
2. The policy should be such that in the long run the probability of being ruined is minimized;
3. The policy should be such that the expected growth rate is maximized.

The remarkable facts are that, first, all of the above objectives are equivalent in the sense that each implies the other two, and, second, the only policy which achieves these objectives is that which in every period maximizes the expected logarithm of wealth at the end of that period. Because of these properties, such a policy may be referred to as a growth-optimal policy. The second property above can actually be made even stronger: First, any policy such that $\mathcal{E}(\ln Y) < \ln W$ will ultimately lead to ruin with probability one. Second, let W_n^* be wealth at the end of the nth period under a growth-optimal policy, and let W_n be wealth under any other policy; then, in the long run, the difference between W_n^* and W_n grows beyond limits with probability one for every policy not asymptotically close to the growth-optimal policy. Thus, in the long run, a growth-optimal policy is infinitely better than any alternative policy.

In addition to these properties, the growth-optimal policy is *myopic* in the sense that today's decision requires information on conditions in the immediate period only [7]. Because of the difficulties involved in estimating probability distributions for share prices in the future, this is a vital property. The main disadvantage—at least at present—of the growth-optimal policy as compared, e.g., with the selection of an E, S efficient policy, is the formidable computational problem.

3.7.   We shall now go one step further in the generalization of our model, and also make a slight change in its formulation. The generalization consists in introducing a nonzero (i.e., a not necessarily zero) interest rate on the riskless asset. The reformulation is caused by the desirability of introducing share prices explicitly into the model. So far we have considered the investment decision in terms of the dollar amount invested; we now want to factor this amount into the number of shares bought and the price per share. This will also mean that we have to reformulate the return on the risky asset in terms of the final value per share. Thus, the new variables entering the model are:

r—interest factor on the riskless asset, i.e., r is one plus the interest rate;

p—current price per share;

X—final value per share (in dollars, including any dividend), with mean μ and variance σ^2;

z—number of shares bought;

$m = W - pz$—dollar investment in riskless asset (net lending).

In some contexts it is more natural to choose units of measurement for p, X, and z more directly related to total company figures. This would mean defining p as the current value of equity of the company, X as the future (random) value of equity, including any dividend, and z as the fraction of equity owned by the investor. Obviously, if a company has one million shares outstanding with a current price of \$20 per share, it is immaterial

whether I say that I own 1000 shares @ $20 or that I have a one-tenth of
1 per cent interest in a company worth $20 million; it costs me $20,000
either way.

The investment in the riskless asset will now grow to rm, while the
final value of the shares will be zX, so that total final wealth is $Y = rm + zX$.
Substituting for the definition of m, we can write this as

$$Y = rW + z(X - rp).$$

Here rW is the value of final wealth that would have been obtained if everything had been invested in the riskless asset, while $X - rp$ is the (random)
excess return from buying a share rather than putting the money in a savings
account.

Expected utility is

$$U = \mathcal{E}[u(Y)] = \sum_x u(rW + z(x - rp)) f(x)$$

so that

$$\frac{dU}{dz} = \mathcal{E}[u'(Y)(X - rp)] = \sum_x u'(rW + z(x - rp))(x - rp) f(x).$$

As before, the second derivative is negative. It is easy to see that a necessary
and sufficient condition for buying a positive number of shares is that
$\mu - rp > 0$. This difference is referred to as the *risk margin* since it defines
the expected return per share over and beyond the return on the same
amount invested in the riskless asset. The condition can be written $\mu/p > r$,
with the interpretation that the expected rate of return from investing in
shares must exceed the interest earned on the riskless asset. Written alternatively as $p < \mu/r$, the condition says that the price per share must be below
the expected present value of the future share price.

3.8. When there is only one risky asset, and all investors agree on
the estimate of μ, the market must necessarily determine a price such that
$p < \mu/r$, because otherwise nobody would hold it and demand could not
equal supply. However, our investor may disagree with the market valuation
and think that the stock is overvalued, i.e., that $p > \mu/r$. He may therefore
wish to consider taking a short position in the stock by selecting a $z < 0$.
Our model is not correctly specified for this case, since our formulation
implies that the value of the short sale would be released for investment in
the riskless asset. In the real world, however, the amount will be tied up until
the investor delivers the shares sold short, and the broker will usually even
require a margin above that to safeguard his position in case the price goes
up. This means that the investor does not earn interest on the amount of
short sales and margin for the period of investment, which clearly makes

a short position less attractive. Disregarding margins above the amount of the short sale, we see that for $z < 0$, $Y = rW + z(X - p)$. In that case, $dU/dz = \mathcal{E}[u'(Y)(X - p)]$. Evaluated at $z = 0$, this derivative is $u'(rW)(\mu - p)$. Thus, the condition for $z < 0$ to be optimal is that $p > \mu$. This will mean that there is a *range* of prices

$$\mu/r < p < \mu$$

between the discounted and the undiscounted expected value of the stock, where $z = 0$ is the optimal solution. Of course, if an additional margin is required, the price must be even higher to induce a short position.

3.9. We shall now proceed on the assumption that $p < \mu/r$, so that the condition for maximum expected utility can be written

(7) $$\mathcal{E}[u'(Y)(X - rp)] = 0.$$

Consider again the case of a quadratic utility function. Then (7) becomes

$$\mathcal{E}[(1 - 2cY)(X - rp)] = \mu - rp - 2c\mathcal{E}(YX) + 2crp\mathcal{E}(Y) = 0.$$

Here $\mathcal{E}(YX) = rW\mu + z(\mu^2 + \sigma^2 - rp\mu)$ and $\mathcal{E}(Y) = rW + z(\mu - rp)$; this gives

$$(\mu - rp)(1 - 2crW) - 2cz[\sigma^2 + (\mu - rp)^2] = 0$$

with the solution

(8) $$z = \frac{\mu - rp}{\sigma^2 + (\mu - rp)^2} (1/2\,c - rW).$$

The similarity with equation (5) is obvious.

Suppose again $c = 1/1000$, $W = \$200$, $r = 1.1$, $p = \$1$, and a distribution of X as

x	$f(x)$
0	1/2
3	1/2

so that $\mu = 1.5$, $\sigma = 1.5$. Except for the interest rate of 10 per cent, these figures correspond exactly to those given in the numerical example above. The solution here becomes $z = 46.5$, which is also the amount of the investment. If we set $r = 1$, the solution will be $z = 60$, as under the earlier formulation.

3.10. There is another way in which our approach to the portfolio selection problem differs from the usual development of the theory. Our approach involves a one-step procedure whereby the optimal portfolio is determined directly as the one which maximizes expected utility. The usual approach, however, breaks the selection procedure down into two steps, involving first an elimination of certain attainable portfolios to form a set of *efficient* portfolios, and then—at least in principle—a final selection of a portfolio from among the efficient ones. Since the pioneering work by Markowitz [6] took this approach, we shall refer to it as the Markowitz procedure.

By an efficient portfolio is invariably meant a portfolio such that its final value has the smallest possible standard deviation S for its level of expectation E (or, alternatively, the largest possible E for the level of S). Thus, the first step in the Markowitz procedure can be explained as follows: Consider any given portfolio with an expected final value of E. By substituting different assets, we shall be able to find a number of other portfolios with the same mean. However, each of these alternative portfolios will normally differ with respect to their standard deviation, so from among these we select the one with the smallest standard deviation. When this computation is repeated for other values of the mean, we obtain a family of portfolios which we can represent in implicit form by a relation

$$g(E, S) = 0$$

describing efficient portfolios. Geometrically, this process is usually illustrated as in Figure 2; the shaded area represents the set of attainable E, S combinations, while the curve defining its south-east boundary repre-

FIGURE 2

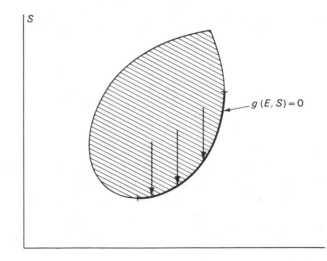

sents the locus of efficient portfolios. The vertical arrows illustrate the minimization of S for any given level of E.

The calculation of efficient portfolios as described above is premeditated on the assumption that the investor is satisfied to use an E, S criterion as discussed in Chapter II, i.e., that the preferred portfolio is one that maximizes some function

$$U = f(E, S).$$

The second step of the Markowitz procedure would therefore consist in calculating the maximum of $U = f(E, S)$ subject to the "efficiency condition" $g(E, S) = 0$. This step could again be illustrated by a diagram with indifference curves over E, S combinations; in Figure 3 the optimal portfolio is represented by the point P where the efficiency locus is tangent to an indifference curve.

FIGURE 3

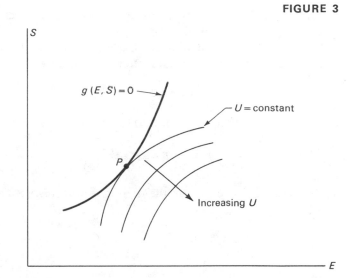

The rationale behind the determination of a set of efficient portfolios would seem to be that for any reasonable preference ordering, the most preferred portfolio will also be an efficient portfolio. Different investors may prefer different portfolios, but they will all be represented by points along the efficiency locus.

It may be useful to illustrate the application of the Markowitz procedure in terms of our portfolio selection model. Actually, with only two assets, the first step of the procedure becomes rather trivial, because once we specify the expected value of the portfolio, the portfolio itself, and hence also its standard deviation, is uniquely determined. This means that no real minimization of S is involved, so that the set of efficient portfolios coincides with the set of attainable ones. To see this, we note that

$$E = rW + z(\mu - rp)$$
$$S = \sigma z.$$

Therefore, any value of E determines z uniquely as

$$z = \frac{E - rW}{\mu - rp}$$

so that the "efficiency" locus is given by

(9) $$S = \frac{\sigma}{\mu - rp}(E - rW)$$

In contrast to the usual picture (Fig. 2), this is seen to represent a straight line intersecting the E axis at $E = rW$.

To be consistent with our model, we have to assume that the preference ordering over E, S combinations is given by

$$U = E - c(E^2 + S^2),$$

or, upon substitution of S from (9),

$$U = E - c\left[E^2 + \frac{\sigma^2}{(\mu - rp)^2}(E - rW)^2\right].$$

To find the maximum, we set the derivative with respect to E equal to zero and solve:

$$\frac{dU}{dE} = 1 - 2c\left[E + \frac{\sigma^2}{(\mu - rp)^2}(E - rW)\right] = 0$$

so that

$$z = \frac{E - rW}{\mu - rp} = \frac{\mu - rp}{\sigma^2 + (\mu - rp)^2}(1/2c - rW)$$

as we have already found out.

3.11. From certain points of view, the Markowitz procedure may seem somewhat complicated or inefficient. It involves a process of computing first and thinking afterwards which means that most of the computational work that goes into determination of the efficiency locus will be wasted; once a particular point on the locus is selected, the rest of it is useless knowledge. This implies that the Markowitz procedure becomes computationally inferior when compared to a direct, one-step procedure.

On the other hand, there are several obvious reasons for the popularity of the Markowitz procedure. The first step of the procedure involves essentially routine, mechanical computation work, whereas the second requires specification of the investor's subjective preferences with respect to risk and expected return. The mere possibility of such a breakdown may have certain advantages. Historically, at the time when Markowitz' work appeared, the expected utility theorem was probably considered controversial. Hence it was natural to take an approach which did not seem to involve a definite stand on the problem of representation of preferences. In effect, it was probably felt that determination of a set of efficient portfolios served to separate facts from opinion. As we have seen, however, such a view is actually misleading, since application of an E, S criterion has itself rather strong implications concerning the nature of the investor's preferences.

Another advantage of the decomposition of the decision process is the division of labor that the procedure allows. From the point of view of the principle of comparative advantage, it may be perfectly rational to leave the computational work to a computer and let the decision maker concentrate on the decision making, even if some work will be wasted. There may also be reasons why the decision maker does not wish to let information on his preferences leak out, and therefore prefers the Markowitz procedure to a direct procedure that would require him to make his preferences explicit to the computer programmer.

Finally, just as the Markowitz procedure requires calculations that will not be needed, the direct procedure requires specification of preferences over probability distributions which may not, after all, be attainable. So perhaps the question really is, what is considered most difficult: to compute or to state preferences? Many people will feel more comfortable in doing computations than in stating a complete and consistent preference ordering. They may feel that once they have a graph of the efficiency locus to look at, the actual decision situation may seem clearer and more manageable.

3.12.   The last step in generalizing our portfolio selection model is to allow more than just one risky stock. We shall now assume that there are n different companies, labeled $j = 1, \ldots, n$, whose shares are offered in the market. Apart from the increase in the number of decision variables, the main new consideration in this case is the stochastic dependence among the yields of different shares. As we shall see, however, the analogy with the one-stock model is extremely close.

   To differentiate among the characteristics of the shares of different companies, we add subscripts to the relevant variables. Thus, X_j, p_j, and z_j now represent the final value, the price, and the amount bought, of the shares of company j. Further, we let μ_j stand for the mean of X_j, and σ_{jk} for the covariance between X_j and X_k, i.e.,

$$\sigma_{jk} = \mathcal{E}(X_j - \mu_j)(X_k - \mu_k).$$

   3.13.   As long as we considered only a single random variable X, it was natural to describe the uncertainty in terms of a probability distribution $f(x)$. When the yield of several different stocks are introduced, a somewhat different formulation has certain advantages. The idea is best illustrated by an example involving the shares of two companies. The value of the shares of company 1, X_1, will be either 0 or 1 with equal probability. If $X_1 = 0$, then $X_2 = 1$ with certainty, while if $X_1 = 1$, then $X_2 = 1$ or $X_2 = 2$, again with equal probability. This situation may be represented diagrammatically by means of the *probability tree* in Figure 4.

FIGURE 4

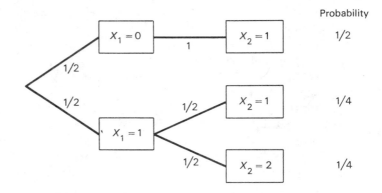

   There are three different branches through this tree, each corresponding to a particular combination of outcomes of X_1 and X_2. The probability of each combination is given at the right. Thus, specifying any particular branch through the tree is equivalent to a complete specification of the outcomes for both variables. It is then natural to label each branch for identification purposes, and we shall call such a label a *state of the world* (or state of nature) and denote it by θ. Thus, in the example, we have (arbitrarily) labeled the branches consecutively from top to bottom, so that θ takes on the values 1, 2, or 3. The information contained in Figure 4 can now be converted into a table giving the value of X_1 and X_2 for each state of the world:

X_j	$\theta = 1$	$\theta = 2$	$\theta = 3$
X_1	0	1	1
X_2	1	1	2
Prob.	1/2	1/4	1/4

Such a tabulation suggests that rather than considering X_1 and X_2 as the basic random variables, we take θ as the (single) basic random variable, and consider X_1 and X_2 as *functions* of θ. Thus, the first two lines in the table give these functional relationships, while the last line defines the probability distribution for θ, which we may denote by $f(\theta)$.

These conventions allow a certain simplification in analytical work; for example, we can now write the mean of X_1 as

$$\mu_1 = \sum_\theta X_1(\theta) f(\theta).$$

If, instead, a formulation in terms of a joint probability distribution for X_1 and X_2, $f(x_1, x_2)$ had been adopted, the expression would have been

$$\mu_1 = \sum_{x_1} \sum_{x_2} x_1 f(x_1, x_2),$$

involving a double sum rather than a single one. In the same way, the covariance between X_1 and X_2 can be expressed as

$$\sigma_{12} = \sum_\theta (X_1(\theta) - \mu_1)(X_2(\theta) - \mu_2) f(\theta).$$

The reader unfamiliar with the notion of states of the world should use formulas such as those above to verify that, in the example, the means and covariances are

$$\mu_1 = 1/2 \qquad \mu_2 = 5/4$$
$$\sigma_{11} = 1/4 \qquad \sigma_{12} = 1/8$$
$$\sigma_{21} = 1/8 \qquad \sigma_{22} = 3/16$$

3.14. We now return to the specification of the portfolio problem. In the budget equation, we have to sum up the amounts $p_j z_j$ to get the total expenditure on shares; therefore

$$W = m + \sum_j p_j z_j,$$

where W and m have the same meaning as before. Similarly, final wealth now comes from $n + 1$ different sources—rm from the riskless asset and $z_j X_j$ from each of the various stocks. Thus,

$$Y = rm + \sum_j z_j X_j,$$

which, upon substitution from the budget equation, can be written as

$$Y = rW + \sum_j z_j(X_j - rp_j).$$

Finally, expected utility becomes

$$U = \mathcal{E}[u(Y)] = \sum_\theta u(rW + \sum_j z_j(X_j(\theta) - rp_j))f(\theta).$$

If no restrictions on margin and short sales are effective, the first-order conditions for a maximum of U are

(10) $$\frac{\partial U}{\partial z_j} = \mathcal{E}[u'(Y)(X_j - rp_j)]$$

$$= \sum_\theta u'(rW + \sum_j z_j(X_j(\theta) - rp_j))(X_j(\theta) - rp_j)f(\theta) = 0$$

$$(j = 1, \ldots, n)$$

Each of these equations looks very much like the optimality condition in the one-share case; in reality, of course, they are quite a bit more complicated, because the expression for Y is more complicated. One immediate consequence is that it is no longer possible with a general utility function to draw any simple conclusions about the conditions under which a particular stock will or will not be held in a positive quantity. Such conditions can still be stated in terms of the various partial derivatives evaluated at $z_j = 0$; the trouble is that this evaluation is no longer straightforward, because even if a particular z_j equals zero, the others may not, and hence Y is still random. Therefore, simple conditions corresponding to that obtained in the one-share case are no longer available. This is not surprising, since we would expect the conditions in the multi-share case to depend on the nature of the stochastic dependence among shares. Thus, for example, if two stocks are negatively correlated, it may well be optimal to hold both in positive quantities, even if one of the risk premiums is negative. Of course, in the case of stochastic independence, the conclusion that z_j is of the same sign as $\mu_j - rp$ remains intact.

3.15.   To explore the application of the conditions (10), we shall again consider the case of a quadratic utility function. With $u' = 1 - 2cY$,

(10) takes the form

$$\mathcal{E}[(1 - 2cY)(X_j - rp_j)] = 0,$$

or

(11) $$\mu_j - rp_j - 2c[\mathcal{E}(YX_j) - rp_j\mathcal{E}(Y)] = 0.$$

We have here

$$\mathcal{E}(Y) = rW + \sum_j z_j(\mu_j - rp_j)$$

$$\mathcal{E}(YX_j) = rW\mu_j + \mathcal{E}[X_j \sum_k z_k(X_k - rp_k)].$$

In evaluating the last expectation, we need the identity $\mathcal{E}(X_jX_k) = \sigma_{jk} + \mu_j\mu_k$; we then have

$$\begin{aligned}
\mathcal{E}[X_j \sum_k z_k(X_k - rp_k)] &= \mathcal{E}[\sum_k z_k(X_jX_k - rp_kX_j)] \\
&= \sum_k z_k[\mathcal{E}(X_jX_k) - rp_k\mathcal{E}(X_j)] \\
&= \sum_k z_k[\sigma_{jk} + \mu_j\mu_k - rp_k\mu_j] \\
&= \sum_k z_k[\sigma_{jk} + \mu_j(\mu_k - rp_k)].
\end{aligned}$$

With these results substituted in (11), we obtain, after collecting terms,

$$(\mu_j - rp_j)(1 - 2crW) - 2c \sum_k z_k[\sigma_{jk} + (\mu_j - rp_j)(\mu_k - rp_k)] = 0$$

which is convenient to write in the form

(12) $$\sum_k z_k[\sigma_{jk} + (\mu_j - rp_j)(\mu_k - rp_k)] = (\mu_j - rp_j)(1/2c - rW)$$

$$(j = 1, \ldots, n)$$

The equations (12) may seem formidable at first look, but we have really obtained a quite simple set of equations, since they constitute a system of n linear equations in n unknowns. A tenth grader can solve them for $n = 2$, and for larger n a computer does it in a matter of milliseconds. The similarity with the optimality condition (8) for the one-share case is quite clear; indeed, for $n = 1$, (12) reduces precisely to

$$z[\sigma^2 + (\mu - rp)^2] = (\mu - rp)(1/2c - rW)$$

with the solution (8).

74916

3.16. To illustrate the solution procedure, suppose the means and covariances are as in the numerical example just discussed; further, let $p_1 = 3/10$, $p_2 = 11/10$, $r = 1$, so that

$$\mu_1 - rp_1 = 1/5, \qquad \mu_2 - rp_2 = 3/20$$

and finally let $W = 500$, $1/2c = 1090$, so that $1/2c - rW = 590$. The coefficients on the LHS of (12) are then

$$\begin{pmatrix} \frac{1}{4} + \left(\frac{1}{5}\right)^2 & \frac{1}{8} + \left(\frac{2}{10}\right)\left(\frac{3}{20}\right) \\ \frac{1}{8} + \left(\frac{2}{10}\right)\left(\frac{3}{20}\right) & \frac{3}{16} + \left(\frac{3}{20}\right)^2 \end{pmatrix} = \begin{pmatrix} \frac{58}{200} & \frac{31}{200} \\ \frac{31}{200} & \frac{42}{200} \end{pmatrix}$$

so that equations (12) become

$$\frac{58}{200} z_1 + \frac{31}{200} z_2 = \frac{1}{5} \cdot 590$$

$$\frac{31}{200} z_1 + \frac{x^2}{200} z_2 = \frac{3}{20} \cdot 590$$

The optimal number of shares to buy are then

$$z_1 = 300, \qquad z_2 = 200.$$

The cost of these shares will be \$310, so that \$190 is put in the savings account. Final wealth will therefore be

$$Y = 190 + 300x_1 + 200x_2$$

which has the distribution

θ	$Y(\theta)$	$f(\theta)$
1	390	1/2
2	690	1/4
3	890	1/4

with a mean of 590 and a variance of 45,000.

3.17. Equations (12) have an interesting property. We notice that the only way in which characteristics of the investor himself (c and W) enter is through a constant factor on the RHS. Now it is well known that multiplying the RHS of a system of linear equations by a constant factor changes the solution of the system by the same factor. This means that if z_j^* is the solution of

$$(13) \qquad \sum_k z_k[\sigma_{jk} + (\mu_j - rp_j)(\mu_k - rp_k)] = \mu_j - rp_j \qquad (j = 1, \ldots, n)$$

then the solution of (12) must be

$$z_j = (1/2c - rW)z_j^*.$$

Now suppose I am an investment counselor guiding my clients in regard to what kinds of portfolios they should hold. I do not need to solve equations (12) each time a client comes through the door; rather, I can solve equations (13) once and thus establish a kind of "reference portfolio" z_j^*. All I have to do with a new client is find out how much money her husband left her and something about her attitude to risk so that the factor $1/2c - rW$ can be determined. Then the portfolio I recommend is obtained by multiplying each of the elements of the reference portfolio by that factor. In the numerical example, the reference portfolio would be

$$z_1^* = \tfrac{30}{59} \qquad z_2^* = \tfrac{20}{59}.$$

3.18.   In the one-share model we found that the E, S efficiency locus was a straight line. We shall now show that this property also holds for the multi-share case. It is difficult to do this in a reasonably compact manner without using some simple matrix notation. The mean and the variance of final wealth are

$$E = rW + \sum_j z_j(\mu_j - rp_j)$$
$$S^2 = \sum_j \sum_k z_j z_k \sigma_{jk}.$$

Defining the column vectors

$$m = \{\mu_j - rp_j\}$$
$$z = \{z_j\}$$

and the covariance matrix

$$C = \{\sigma_{jk}\}$$

we can write

$$E = rW + m'z$$
$$S^2 = z'Cz.$$

An efficient portfolio is one which minimizes S^2 at any given level of E; to determine the efficient portfolios we therefore form the Lagrangean

$$L = z'Cz - \lambda(E - rW - m'z),$$

where λ is a (scalar) Langrange multiplier. Setting the derivatives with respect to the z_j equal to zero, we have the optimality conditions

$$\frac{\partial L}{\partial z} = 2Cz - \lambda m = 0,$$

or

$$Cz = \frac{\lambda}{2} m.$$

Assuming that C is nonsingular (no linear dependence among yields), we can solve for z as

(14) $z = \frac{\lambda}{2} C^{-1}m.$

With this solution we have

$$E - rW = \frac{\lambda}{2} m'C^{-1}m$$

$$S^2 = \left(\frac{\lambda}{2}\right)^2 m'C^{-1}m$$

(since C, and so also C^{-1}, are symmetric). Eliminating $\lambda/2$ between these equations, we obtain

$$S = k(E - rW),$$

where $k = (m'C^{-1}m)^{-1/2}$. Hence the E, S efficiency locus is a straight line intersecting the E axis at $E = rW$.

Applying these results to our numerical example, we find

$$C^{-1} = \begin{pmatrix} 6 & -4 \\ -4 & 8 \end{pmatrix}$$

so that

$$m'C^{-1}m = \left(\frac{1}{5}, \frac{3}{20}\right)\begin{pmatrix} 6 & -4 \\ -4 & 8 \end{pmatrix}\begin{pmatrix} \frac{1}{5} \\ \frac{3}{20} \end{pmatrix} = \frac{9}{50}.$$

Thus, the efficiency locus is given by

$$S = 2.357(E - 500)$$

The reader can easily verify that maximizing $U = E - (E^2 + S^2)/2180$ subject to this condition gives $E = 590$, $S^2 = 45,000$, as we found directly above.

3.19. The assumption that the covariance matrix is nonsingular is actually quite innocuous. Singularity would imply that the yield on one share, say X_r, is a linear combination of returns on other shares; this would mean that the probability distribution of return for a portfolio using share r can be exactly replicated by substituting for share r the corresponding subportfolio of shares of which share r is a linear combination. This means that although the z_j may not be uniquely determined, the portfolio's probability distribution is; hence all properties of the portfolio remain intact.

Note also that there is no inconsistency between the equations defining an optimal portfolio in the case of quadratic utility functions [equations (12)] and those defining efficient portfolios [equations (14)]. In matrix form, (12) can be written

$$(C + mm')z = \left(\frac{1}{2c} - rW\right) m$$

with solution

$$z = \left(\frac{1}{2c} - rW\right)(C + mm')^{-1}m.$$

It is now a fact that vectors $(C + mm')^{-1}m$ and $C^{-1}m$ are proportional.[2] In our example, the vector $C^{-1}m$ is given by

$$\begin{pmatrix} 6 & -4 \\ -4 & 8 \end{pmatrix}\begin{pmatrix} \frac{1}{5} \\ \frac{3}{20} \end{pmatrix} = \begin{pmatrix} \frac{3}{5} \\ \frac{2}{5} \end{pmatrix}$$

implying that the risky assets in any efficient portfolio are held in the proportion $3:2$, just as in the model with quadratic utility functions. This confirms the intuitive proposition that any portfolio which maximizes the expectation of a quadratic utility function is efficient and, conversely, any efficient portfolio maximizes the expectation of some quadratic utility function.

3.20. The preceding considerations also indicate that any two investors who choose efficient portfolios will divide the total amount invested in risky assets equally among different assets. That is, if we define

$$\alpha_j = \frac{p_j z_j}{\sum\limits_k p_k z_k}$$

as the fraction of the total amount invested in risky assets that is invested in asset j, then the α_j are the same for all investors. To see this, let z'_j be the solu-

[2]Specifically,

$$(C + mm')^{-1}m = \frac{|C|}{|C+mm'|} C^{-1}m.$$

tion of the equations $z = C^{-1}m$; then $z_j = (\lambda/2)z'_j$. Clearly, the z'_j are the same for all investors (assuming, of course, that their estimates of C and m are the same). Then $p_j z_j = (\lambda/2)p_j z'_j$ and $\sum_k p_k z_k = (\lambda/2)\sum_k p_k z'_k$ and hence

$$\alpha_j = \frac{p_j z'_j}{\sum_k p_k z'_k}$$

for all investors. This is referred to as the separation *property* in portfolio selection, since the decision on the *composition* of the risky part of the portfolio can be separated from the decision on its *size*. In other words, differences in preferences (risk aversion) are reflected only in the relative sizes of the risky and riskless parts of the portfolio, not in the composition of the risky part. From this point of view it is possible to analyze risk taking behavior in terms of a simple two-asset model in which the risky asset is really a mix of different assets whose composition is independent of the investor's preferences.

3.21.   We said above that with a general utility function it is difficult to spell out the conditions for long or short positions in different assets. By restricting attention to E, S efficient portfolios, certain quantitative conditions can be derived, however. From (14) it is clear that the signs of the z_j are the same as the signs of the corresponding elements of the vectors $C^{-1}m$. This is because λ represents the rate of substitution between E and V along the efficiency locus, and hence, by the assumption of risk aversion, must be positive. Letting σ^{jk} be the elements of C^{-1}, the jth element of $C^{-1}m$ can be written in full as

$$\sum_k \sigma^{jk}(\mu_k - rp_k),$$

so that z_j is of the same sign as a certain linear combination of the risk margins. For an arbitrary number of assets such a condition does not seem to allow any intuitive interpretations. For $n = 2$, however, we have

$$C^{-1} = \frac{1}{|C|}\begin{pmatrix} \sigma_{22} & -\sigma_{12} \\ -\sigma_{12} & \sigma_{11} \end{pmatrix}$$

so that

$$C^{-1}m = \frac{1}{|C|}\begin{pmatrix} m_1\sigma_{22} - m_2\sigma_{12} \\ m_2\sigma_{11} - m_1\sigma_{12} \end{pmatrix}.$$

C being positive definite, the determinant $|C|$ is positive; this means that $z_1 > 0$ if and only if $m_1\sigma_{22} > m_2\sigma_{12}$. Letting σ_j denote the standard deviations $\sigma_{jj}^{1/2}$ and ρ the coefficient of correlation $\sigma_{12}/\sigma_1\sigma_2$, the condition can be written

$$\frac{m_1}{\sigma_1} > \rho \frac{m_2}{\sigma_2}.$$

Similarly, $z_2 > 0$ if and only if

$$\frac{m_2}{\sigma_2} > \rho \frac{m_1}{\sigma_1}.$$

These conditions are illustrated geometrically in Figures 5 and 6 for the cases of ρ positive and negative, respectively.

In the case of negative correlation we see, for example, that both z_j may be positive even though one of the risk margins is negative. Of course, this case is not very interesting from a practical point of view, since negatively correlated assets are extremely rare in the real world.

In the more realistic case of $\rho > 0$ we note that it may be optimal to take a short position in one asset even if its risk margin is positive (short positions for asset 1 or asset 2 in the sectors labeled a and b, respectively). In addition, the more strongly the assets are correlated, the greater the likelihood of this taking place. This fact may have some significance for the theory of financial intermediaries. For example, a finance company typically takes a short position in some securities, such as issue of commercial paper, although the risk premium is obviously positive, to finance a long position

FIGURE 5

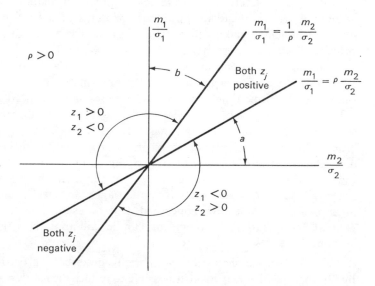

FIGURE 6

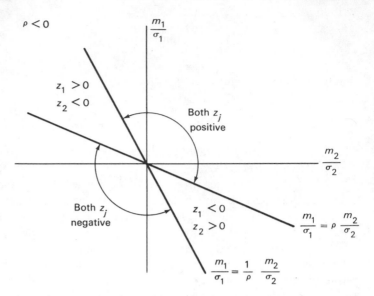

in other assets (extension of loans). Traditional analyses of financial intermediaries seem to have missed such relationships between the yields on
securities in long and short positions by treating management of items on the
asset side of the balance sheet and those on the liability side as completely
separate problems. We shall not pursue these ideas further, but refer to the
study by Pyle [8].

3.22. Selection of an efficient portfolio requires quite a large
amount of input in the form of estimates of all the μ_j and σ_{jk}. We shall not go
into the problem of making these estimates in any detail. Most empirical work
concerned with such estimates has been based on historical data on price
movements in the stock market, i.e., time series data have been used for
estimating a vector of means and a covariance matrix for returns on selected
shares. At the same time, it seems to be increasingly realized that estimates
based on historical data may have little or no relevance for predicting future
stock price behavior. Although there are still people who earn a living by
looking at charts, the general trend in security analysis seems to be in the
direction of careful analysis of underlying economic conditions—both on
the level of particular industries or the economy as a whole, and on the level
of the individual company's relative potential as far as technology, marketing,
or administrative talent are concerned. It is no use to pretend that anything
general, yet operationally significant, can be said about how this task should
be done.

3.23. We shall, however, briefly describe a procedure suggested
by Sharpe [9] which may make it possible to reduce the *number* of independent

·estimates that have to be made. Since we do not get something for nothing, this requires certain restrictive assumptions about the nature of the stochastic dependence among stocks.

Sharpe's model essentially makes two kinds of assumptions. The first is that each X_j can be decomposed into two components, say $X_j = Z_j + Q_j$, such that the components Z_j are perfectly correlated with each other, while the Q_j are independent of each other. Thus, Z_j represents the part of X_j which moves with the rest of the market as a result of the general level of economic activity, while Q_j represents the deviations of X_j from the common trend, and thus reflects the uniqueness of company j. The decomposition is assumed to be such that $\mathcal{E}(Q_j) = 0$, and the independence assumption implies $\mathcal{E}(Q_j Q_k) = 0$. The second assumption concerns the specification of Z_j as a linear function of some "market indicator" X, i.e.,

$$Z_j = \alpha_j + \beta_j X.$$

A natural measure of X might just be the sum of the X_j, or some other stock market or economic index. Smith [10] has studied the performance of a number of such indexes for application in the Sharpe model. The assumption of linearity is probably more for mathematical simplicity than for theoretical reasons.

Denote the variance of Q_j by V_j, and the mean and variance of X by E and V. It is further assumed that Q_j is independent of X, i.e., $\mathcal{E}[Q_j(X - E) = 0$. Under these assumptions we have

$$\mu_j = \mathcal{E}(X_j) = \mathcal{E}(\alpha_j + \beta_j X + Q_j)$$
$$= \alpha_j + \beta_j E$$

so that $X_j - \mu_j = \beta_j(E - X) + Q_j$. Then, for $k \neq j$, we have

$$\sigma_{jk} = \mathcal{E}(X_j - \mu_j)(X_k - \mu_k)$$
$$= \mathcal{E}[\beta_j(E - X) + Q_j][\beta_k(E - X) + Q_k]$$
$$= \mathcal{E}[\beta_j\beta_k(E - X)^2 + \beta_j Q_k(E - X) + \beta_k Q_j(E - X) + Q_j Q_k]$$
$$= \beta_j\beta_k V$$

since the expectation of the last three terms are all zero. For the variance we obtain

$$\sigma_{jj} = \mathcal{E}(X_j - \mu_j)^2$$
$$= \mathcal{E}[\beta_j(X - E) + Q_j]^2$$
$$= \mathcal{E}[\beta_j^2(X - E)^2 + 2\beta_j Q_j(X - E) + Q_j^2]$$
$$= \beta_j^2 V + V_j$$

since the middle term vanishes.

This model may allow a substantial decrease in the number of estimates required. To obtain the μ_j and σ_{jk} directly requires $n + n(n + 1)/2$ idenpendent estimates, while the Sharpe model requires just $3n + 2$ estimates: α_j, β_j, and V_j for each stock, and E and V. For ten stocks the numbers are 65 vs. 32, and for 100 stocks 5,150 vs. 302. Furthermore, the α_j, β_j, and V_j may be estimated routinely from time series data and still be quite reliable, so that the estimates that require real skill are those of E and V. With the amount of econometric forecasting being done these days, even those estimates may not be so hard to come up with. We shall return to an application of the Sharpe model in a later chapter.

3.24.   A substantial part of the theory to be developed in this book is based on the assumption that investors choose E, S efficient portfolios. If we allow investors to have arbitrary utility functions, there is in general no reason to expect their optimal portfolios to be efficient. On the other hand, it does seem intuitively reasonable to expect the portfolios to be fairly *close* to the efficiency locus. The empirical validity of our theory will therefore depend on how closely efficiency is approximated in real world portfolios. Suppose, for example, that an investor pursues a growth-optimal policy, implying maximization of the expected logarithm of wealth; is his behavior going to be significantly different from that of an investor selecting his portfolio on the basis of E, S efficiency? At present, no easy answer to such questions seems available, although some general ideas suggest themselves.

Hakansson [5] has presented some simple numerical examples which seem to indicate that a growth-optimal portfolio may actually be quite far away from E, S efficiency. However, the examples involve a very small number of securities (two or three), whereas most real portfolios contain a fairly large number of securities, so the examples are somewhat inconclusive.

If the probability distribution for final wealth is fully described by just two parameters, then any optimal portfolio—regardless of the utility function—will be efficient. Now we would expect almost any reasonable utility function to induce a fairly well diversified portfolio; indeed, we know this to be a real world fact. There is also both theoretical and empirical evidence that the distribution of returns on well diversified portfolios can be satisfactorily described by two-parameter distributions. If this evidence is accepted, it would follow that any optimal portfolio is very close to the efficiency locus, and hence the efficiency assumption is much less restrictive than it may appear at first.

3.25.   The theoretical argument would in some way appeal to the central limit theorem: With a well diversified portfolio final wealth is the sum of many separate assets, hence its distributions will tend towards normality. However, a number of the assumptions on the probability distributions for individual assets ordinarily required for the central limit theorem to hold may not be satisfied, and the argument is therefore somewhat inconclusive. Individual asset returns are neither independently nor identically distributed, and in such cases little is known about whether a limiting distribution exists, and less is known about the rate of convergence. Even more serious is the possibility that the variances of return on individual shares may not exist. Fama [3] has presented empirical analyses of return distributions which indicate that they may belong to a class of distributions (called *stable*, or *Paretian*, distributions) whose variances are infinite. However, these studies are based on analyses of individual share prices and the probability distributions in question are therefore to be considered as the *marginal* distributions of some joint probability distribution. The problem is finding what happens to a sum of stochastically dependent random variables whose marginal distributions have infinite variances. On the theoretical level we know nothing about this problem, although we cannot rule out the possibility that such a portfolio would be approximately normally distributed. To throw some light on it we shall examine some data on portfolio returns presented by Fisher and Lorie [4].

   3.26.   The basic data (Fisher and Lorie's Table A1) consist of statistics on wealth ratios (i.e., the ratio between final and initial wealth) for portfolios of 1, 2, 8, 16, 32, and 128 stocks listed on the NYSE. For one- and two-stock portfolios, the distribution of wealth ratios for all possible combinations of stocks are tabulated, while the data for larger portfolios are based on large random samples. All portfolios consist of equal investment in each stock. The statistics given are the 5th, 10th, 20th, . . . , 90th, and 95th centiles of the frequency distributions, as well as various measures of location and dispersion, including the mean and standard deviation. As an example, consider the frequency distribution for portfolios consisting of 8, 32, and 128 stocks for the year 1965 (Table 1).

   In this table we have compared the statistics of the observed frequencies with the corresponding statistics for a normal distribution with the same means and standard deviations. The differences between the observed and the normal statistics thus give indications of the goodness of fit of the observed distributions to normality. It is seen that for all statistics listed (except, of course, the mean and standard deviation, which are equal by assumption) the agreement with the normal statistics increases with the number of stocks in the portfolio. Even for portfolios containing 8 and 32 stocks the agreement with normal distributions seems quite good, and for portfolios containing 128 stocks the similarity with a normal distribution is so close that for all practical purposes they can be considered identical. Corresponding calculations for other years in the period 1926–1965 give similar results, and the figures in Table 1 can therefore be considered fully representative.

TABLE 1

Frequency Distributions of Wealth Ratios from Investments in Randomly
Selected Portfolios Containing Specified Numbers of Stocks Listed
on the NYSE, 12/31/64–12/31/65, Compared to Normal Distributions
with the Same Means and Standard Deviations*

Statistic	$N = 8$ Observed	Normal	$N = 32$ Observed	Normal	$N = 128$ Observed	Normal
5th centile	1.081	1.046	1.174	1.167	1.227	1.226
10th centile	1.117	1.098	1.195	1.192	1.239	1.238
20th centile	1.163	1.161	1.222	1.223	1.253	1.253
30th centile	1.200	1.207	1.243	1.246	1.263	1.264
40th centile	1.232	1.246	1.261	1.265	1.272	1.273
50th centile	1.264	1.282	1.278	1.283	1.281	1.282
60th centile	1.299	1.318	1.296	1.301	1.290	1.291
70th centile	1.338	1.357	1.316	1.329	1.300	1.300
80th centile	1.389	1.403	1.340	1.343	1.311	1.311
90th centile	1.467	1.466	1.376	1.374	1.328	1.326
95th centile	1.543	1.518	1.409	1.399	1.341	1.338
Mean	1.282	1.282	1.283	1.282	1.282	1.282
Standard deviation	.144	.144	.071	.071	.034	.034
Mean deviation	.111	.115	.056	.057	.027	.027
Gini's mean difference	.158	.163	.080	.080	.039	.038
Skewness	.887	.000	.445	.000	.177	.000
Kurtosis	4.654	3.000	3.444	3.000	2.958	3.000

*From data in Table A1, Fisher and Lorie [4].

The data thus seem to support the hypothesis that returns on well diversified portfolios are approximately normally distributed, and hence appear to favor the assumption that investors' portfolio choices are mean-variance efficient.

REFERENCES

1. Arrow, K. J. *Aspects of the Theory of Risk-Bearing*. Helsinki: The Yrjö Jahnsson Foundation, 1965.
2. Breiman, L. "Optimal Gambling Systems for Favorable Games," *Fourth Berkeley Symposium on Mathematical Statistics and Probability*, Berkeley, California, 1961.

3. Fama, E. F. "The Behavior of Stock Market Prices," *Jour. Bus.*, 1965, pp. 34–105.
4. Fisher, L., and J. H. Lorie. "Some Studies of Variability of Returns on Investments in Common Stocks," *Jour. Bus.*, 1970, pp. 99–134.
5. Hakansson, N. H. "Capital Growth and the Mean-Variance Approach to Portfolio Selection," *Jour. Fin. Quant. Anal.*, 1971, pp. 517–557.
6. Markowitz, H. M. "Portfolio Selection," *Jour. Finance*, 1952, pp. 77–91.
7. Mossin, J. "Optimal Multiperiod Portfolio Policies," *Jour. Bus.*, 1968, pp. 215–229.
8. Pyle, D. H. "On the Theory of Financial Intermediation," *Jour. Finance*, 1971, p. 737–747.
9. Sharpe, W. F. "A Simplified Model for Portfolio Analysis," *Mgt. Sci.*, 1963, pp. 277–293.
10. Smith, K. V. "Stock Price and Economic Indexes for Generating Efficient Portfolios," *Jour. Bus.*, 1968, pp. 326–336.
11. Tobin, J. "Liquidity Preference as Behavior towards Risk," *Rev. Econ. Stud.*, 1957–58, pp. 65–86.

4 Security

Market Equilibrium

4.1. Having formulated the relations describing the individual investor's demand for various securities, we are now in a position to put the demand functions of different investors together and construct a general equilibrium model of the pricing and allocation of the given supply of securities. That is, we want to describe the characteristics of a situation in which investors' combined demand is equal to the supply for every security. The pioneering study of security market equilibrium was made by Sharpe [5]. In [3], a restatement and some extensions of his model were given. Portions of this chapter draw heavily on the reformulation of that model presented in [4].

4.2. The model we shall consider is very much in the classical tradition and represents in many ways an extremely simplified picture of real world capital markets. Formally, it is a model of pure exchange, and there are two kinds of exchange objects: promissory notes, which we shall refer to as bonds, carrying a fixed interest rate, and company ordinary shares. Being a pure exchange model, it takes as given the firm's investment and financing decisions. On the basis of the relationships to be derived between these decisions and market values, we can infer the effects of alternative decisions. In Chapter VIII, we shall consider some of the problems concerned with determination of the overall level of activity of the firm.

We shall not discuss in any detail the process, or mechanism, by which an equilibrium position is actually attained. The standard textbook explanation is that the market behaves as if there were a "market manager" to aid in the trading. The market manager announces a set of prices, and each investor can then compute the value of the securities he is currently holding and which in our terms constitutes his initial wealth. Knowing this, he can inform the market manager how much of each security he is prepared to hold at those prices. The market manager then adds up the demand of all investors for each security and compares with the given supply. If demand equals supply for every security, the exchange will be effected; otherwise the market manager announces a new set of prices (presumably by raising relative prices of securities with excess demand), and the process is repeated until equilibrium is reached. Floor trading in actual security markets closely resembles this process, and because of the unusually rapid flow of information, security markets are probably more effective than any other market in eliminating discrepancies between demand and supply.

4.3.   The activity carried out by company j is described by a random variable X_j representing, in some way, the future value of the firm. There are several ways in which we can give concrete meaning to this variable. The simplest conceptually is to consider the firm as a one-period activity to be liquidated at the end of the period; X_j would in this case represent the realized value of its assets at that time. A stylized example may serve to illustrate this interpretation: Each company is a farm which has, at the time of trading, effected its investments (planting of its land) as well as its financing (share sale and borrowing). Thus, the supply of the various securities are given data. Trading then determines an allocation of these securities among investors. Crop values are still unknown and represented by the random variables X_j. After the harvest is completed, the crop values will be used partly for amortizing debt, while the remainder will be distributed to shareholders.

As a model of the real world, the assumption that all firms will be liquidated is obviously not very satisfactory, and a more appealing interpretation is that X_j represents an infinite *flow* of earnings (gross earnings per time unit), in principle stationary through time, but unknown as of the market date.

A third interpretation, theoretically more troublesome, is that investors foresee another trading date in the future at which share prices, depending on the success or failure of the company's operations in the meantime, may be different from what they are today. In this case, X_j would have to be taken as the future value of the company. Obviously, the interpretation of the properties of the model will depend on our interpretation of the variables entering the model. To simplify the exposition, we shall refer to X_j as the (gross) *return* of company j.

Whichever way we choose to interpret the time span of the model, its basic nature is static. That is, we consider the pricing and allocation of securities at some given point in time without explicit recognition of sequential adjustment processes.

4.4. Apart from the specification of investor preferences, our model rests on a number of assumptions with respect to the investors' environment and his perception of it. At this stage we shall state briefly the most important of these assumptions; as we go along we shall examine their role in more detail and see how our conclusions must be modified if these assumptions are relaxed.

One such important assumption is commonly referred to as the *homogeneity of beliefs* assumption. This implies that all investors agree in their estimates of the return prospects for the various securities available, i.e., we assume that all investors base their portfolio decisions on the same estimates of the probability distributions for gross returns X_j.

As far as the returns on individual securities are concerned, we shall assume, at least initially, that *default risk* is never present for either firms or individual investors. All lending, whether to individuals or in the form of corporate bond holdings, is considered as perfectly riskless investment. This implies that all bonds are perfect substitutes for each other, and that it is therefore unnecessary to distinguish among bonds issued by different firms or investors.

Another important assumption is that *security markets are perfect*. We shall define this to mean that any two securities (or combinations of securities) which are perfect substitutes for each other shall cost investors the same amount. This means a number of things. First, it implies the absence of many kinds of transactions costs, so that ten shares cost the investor precisely ten times the cost of one share. It also means that the interest rate on all riskless bonds must be the same; together with the preceding assumption this would imply that all investors and firms can lend or borrow freely at the same riskless interest rate.

Finally we shall—not without a certain loss of generality, but in order to concentrate on theoretical essentials—disregard all forms of taxes.

4.5. The model's variables will be denoted as in the preceding chapter. The only difference is that we now have to add another subscript to some of the variables to distinguish among different investors. Thus, W_i, z_{ij}, m_i, Y_i, and u_i now refer to initial wealth, fraction owned of company j, net lending, final wealth, and the utility function, respectively, for investor i ($i = 1, \ldots, m$). In addition, we introduce company j's debt level, denoted by d_j, and the (total) market value of the company, v_j, defined as the sum of the market value of its equity, p_j, and its debt, i.e., $v_j = p_j + d_j$.

4.6.   It is now a relatively straightforward task to set up the general equilibrium model. For each investor we have the budget equation

$$(1) \qquad\qquad W_i = m_i + \sum_j z_{ij} p_j \qquad\qquad (i = 1, \ldots, m)$$

while his final wealth is given by

$$Y_i = rm_i + \sum_j z_{ij}(X_j - rd_j)$$

where the factors $X_j - rd_j$ are the amounts available to shareholders after principal and interest has been paid on the companies' debt. Upon substitution of m_i from the budget equation, final wealth can be written

$$(2) \qquad\qquad Y_i = rW_i + \sum_j z_{ij}(X_j - rd_j - rp_j)$$
$$= rW_i + \sum_j z_{ij}(X_j - rv_j).$$

From this we see that regardless of the portfolio the investor chooses to buy, the probability distribution for final wealth will depend only on the total value of the companies, not on how these values are composed of equity value and debt.

With the Y_i given by (2), it follows that for each investor the demand relations for shares are given by

$$(3) \qquad\qquad \mathcal{E}[u_i'(Y_i)(X_j - rv_j)] = 0 \qquad (i = 1, \ldots, m, j = 1, \ldots, n)$$

while the budget equation (1) determines his net lending. Equations (1) and (3) constitute, for each investor, $n + 1$ equations to determine the $n + 1$ variables z_{ij} and m_i. Altogether, then, we have $n(m + 1)$ demand equations.

The *market clearing conditions*, guaranteeing equality between demand and supply, are

$$(4) \qquad\qquad \sum_i z_{ij} = 1 \qquad\qquad (j = 1, \ldots, n)$$
$$\sum_i m_i = \sum_j d_j$$

The first set of equations says that all firms must be owned by somebody (the percentage interest of shareholders must add to unity for all firms), and the second says that in the aggregate, investors' net lending must equal the total supply of corporate bonds. This is so because lending and borrowing among investors must cancel; what is borrowed by one must be lent by another. As in any equilibrium model, one of the market clearing conditions is actually superfluous, because, as noted above, initial wealth consists simply of the value, at the ruling market prices, of the investor's initial holdings. Denoting these by $\bar{m}_i$ and $\bar{z}_{ij}$, we thus have as a definition of initial wealth

$$W_i = \bar{m}_i + \sum_j \bar{z}_{ij} p_j.$$

The initial allocation satisfies

$$\sum_i \bar{z}_{ij} = 1 \quad \text{and} \quad \sum_i \bar{m}_i = \sum_j d_j$$

as identities. Thus, $\sum_i W_i = \sum_i \bar{m}_i + \sum_i \sum_j \bar{z}_{ij} p_j = \sum_j d_j + \sum_j p_j = \sum_j v_j$; the sum of investors' wealth is just equal to the total value of firms. Now consider an allocation such that (1) and (4) are all satisfied. Summing (1) over i gives

$$\sum_i m_i + \sum_i \sum_j z_{ij} p_j = \sum_j v_j,$$

which, using (4), implies that $\sum_i m_i = \sum_j d_j$. This means that we have only n independent market clearing conditions.

The complete model thus consists of equations (1), (3), and (4), a system of $m(n + 1) + n$ independent equations. The variables to be determined are the mn variables z_{ij} and the m variables m_i, and the equilibrium prices. In principle, there are $n + 1$ prices in the model: the n share prices p_j and the price $1/r$ for the riskless asset (one unit of money payable with certainty). We see, however, that we have sufficient equations to determine only n of these prices. This means that one of the prices can be determined arbitrarily (the corresponding security is selected as *numéraire*, or unit of measurement for prices), and it is natural to consider the interest rate as being exogenously given. This means that the model is capable of determining ratios between rates of return on different assets, not their absolute value. The situation is the same in the classical theory of commodity exchange—only relative prices can be determined, so the unit of measurement of one commodity has to be chosen as the unit of measurement of the prices of other commodities (the price of meat or bread is expressed as a certain number of candlesticks).

That our model is incapable of determining the interest rate is of course not surprising. The riskless interest rate represents in some sense the "price for waiting," and such a price cannot be determined in a one-period model without physical investment.

4.7.   As it stands, the equilibrium model is obviously too general to yield much in the way of meaningful conclusions. To see its potential for generating operationally significant hypotheses, let us first make the strong assumption that all utility functions are quadratic:

$$u_i(Y_i) = Y_i - c_i Y_i^2 \qquad\qquad (i = 1, \ldots, m)$$

This will make it possible to derive an explicit expression for the market prices, which will depend on expected returns and covariances between returns only.

For the case of a quadratic utility function we have already, in Chapter III, derived the individual investor's demand functions. In the new notation, these take the form

(5)
$$\sum_k z_{ik}[\sigma_{jk} + (\mu_j - rv_j)(\mu_k - rv_k)]$$
$$= (\mu_j - rv_j)(\tfrac{1}{2}c_i - rW_i)$$

where, because of the introduction of corporate debt, p_j has been replaced by v_j. Furthermore, we have also noted that if $z_1^*, z_2^*, \ldots, z_n^*$ is the solution of

$$\sum_k z_k[\sigma_{jk} + (\mu_j - rv_j)(\mu_k - rv_k)] = (\mu_j - rv_j)$$

then the solution of (5) is

(6)
$$z_{ij} = z_j^*(\tfrac{1}{2}c_i - rW_i) \qquad\qquad (j = 1, \ldots, n)$$

Summing in (6) over i therefore gives

$$\sum_i z_{ij} = z_j^* \left(\sum_i \frac{1}{2c_i} - r \sum_i W_i \right),$$

but from the market clearing conditions we know that this sum *must* equal unity. Therefore,

$$z_j^* = \frac{1}{\displaystyle\sum_i \frac{1}{2c_i} - r \sum_i W_i},$$

which, when substituted in (6), gives

(7)
$$z_{ij} = \frac{\dfrac{1}{2c_i} - rW_i}{\displaystyle\sum_i \frac{1}{2c_i} - r \sum_i W_i}.$$

The noteworthy thing about this expression is that the RHS does not depend on j. This means that

$$z_{i1} = z_{i2} = \cdots = z_{in}.$$

In other words, *in equilibrium, any investor holds the same percentage of the outstanding stock of all companies.* This percentage, which we may denote

z_i, will be different for different individuals, but if an investor holds, say, 2 percent of the stock of one company, he also holds 2 percent of the stock of every other company. This property permits us to summarize the description of an investor's portfolio by stating (a) his net lending or borrowing, and (b) the percentage z_i held of all outstanding shares. Note that this property, which is a general equilibrium property, is stronger than the separation property discussed in Chapter III, which holds for any optimal portfolio. We shall refer to a portfolio where $z_{ij} = z_i$ for all j as a *balanced* portfolio.

4.8. Let x_{ij} be the amount invested in company j by investor i. Then $z_{ij} = x_{ij}/p_j$. Then, if the portfolio is balanced, for any two investors r and s and any companies j and k we should have

$$\frac{x_{rj}}{p_j} = \frac{x_{rk}}{p_k}$$

$$\frac{x_{sj}}{p_j} = \frac{x_{sk}}{p_k}$$

and consequently

$$\frac{x_{rj}}{x_{sj}} = \frac{x_{rk}}{x_{sk}}.$$

In other words, the ratio between the holdings of two investors is the same for all shares.

4.9. From the expression (7) it is now obvious that when prices are in equilibrium, no short positions will be taken by any investor. By assumption, all investors operate on the increasing part of their utility function; hence $1/2c_i - rW_i > 0$, and so also is their sum. The underlying reason for this result is the homogeneity of beliefs assumption: A short position will be taken only by an investor who disagrees strongly with the rest of the market.

4.10. The practical-minded reader will rightly object to the extreme degree of diversification implied by the above as quite unreasonable and contrary to fact. We shall, however, derive some other properties of the model before we consider various reasons why such a result may not be expected to hold in practice.

Since the $z_{ik} = z_i$ for all k, they can be moved outside the summation sign in (5); then substituting from (7) and rearranging, we obtain

$$\sum_k [\sigma_{jk} + (\mu_j - rv_j)(\mu_k - rp_k)]$$

$$= (\mu_j - rv_j)\left(\sum_i \frac{1}{2c_i} - r\sum_i W_i\right)$$

or

(8)
$$\sum_k \sigma_{jk} + (\mu_j - rv_j)(\sum_k \mu_k - r \sum_k v_k)$$
$$= (\mu_j - rv_j)\left(\sum_i \frac{1}{2c_i} - r \sum_i W_i\right).$$

As already noted, $\sum_i W_i = \sum_k v_k$; hence the term $r(\mu_j - rv_j)\sum_k p_k$ drops out on both sides, and we are left with

$$\sum_k \sigma_{jk} - (\mu_j - rv_j)\left(\sum_i \frac{1}{2c_i} - \sum_k \mu_k\right) = 0.$$

Solving for v_j then gives

$$v_j = \frac{1}{r}\left(\mu_j - \frac{\sum_k \sigma_{jk}}{\sum_i \frac{1}{2c_i} - \sum_k \mu_k}\right).$$

By defining

$$b_j = \sum_k \sigma_{jk}$$

$$R = \frac{1}{\sum_i \frac{1}{2c_i} - \sum_k \mu_k}$$

we can write the equilibrium value of the firm as

(9)
$$v_j = \frac{1}{r}(\mu_j - Rb_j).$$

Here we have a surprisingly simple formula for the company's market value, expressed solely in terms of given market parameters. Interpretation of the formula is also very simple. The second term (Rb_j) is, as we shall see, a correction term for risk, so the market value is computed simply by taking the expected return, allowing a certain deduction for risk, and then discounting the difference at the riskless interest rate. Note that if we consider the model's time span as infinite, with r being the interest rate, then $1/r$ becomes the appropriate discount factor.

Valuation formulae of the same nature as (9) have of course often been suggested on an ad hoc basis as a "reasonable" way of taking uncertainty into account. Here, however, we have *derived* the formula from more basic assumptions about investors' choices and market arrangements.

The correction term for risk is seen to consist of two factors, R and b_j. Of these, b_j is defined as the sum of company j's covariances of return with all other firms. Thus, in the case of quadratic utilities, this is the relevant risk measure associated with company j's activities. It can be interpreted as the contribution of company j to the market's total variance, since we obviously have

$$\sum_j b_j = \sum_j \sum_k \sigma_{jk} = \mathrm{Var}\left(\sum_j X_j\right).$$

Alternatively, b_j is the covariance between X_j and total market return, i.e.,

$$b_j = \mathrm{Cov}\left(X_j, \sum_k X_k\right),$$

and is therefore occasionally referred to as company j's *systematic risk*. It is not surprising to learn that a company's risk cannot be measured by its own variance (σ_{jj}) alone, but also depends on its correlation with the rest of the economy. In traditional approaches to financial analysis this dependence is often missed, however. Loosely speaking, a rainwear manufacturer is worth relatively more if everybody else produces ice cream and suntan lotion. We even observe that if the return of a company is sufficiently negatively correlated with other companies' returns, then b_j may—at least in principle—become negative. Since holdings in such a company strongly reduce the variances of return on investors' portfolios, demand will be so large as to raise the market value of the company above its expected present value. In practice, of course, such an occurence is highly unlikely.

The other factor, R, is now seen to serve as a weighting factor for the company's risk measure b_j. It is important to note that this weighting factor is the same for all companies and must therefore in some way reflect a "market risk aversion." Such an interpretation can indeed be given; the reader can easily verify that with quadratic utility functions, R can be expressed as

$$R = \frac{1}{\sum_i \mathcal{E}\left(\frac{1}{R_i}\right)}$$

where $R_i(Y_i)$ is investor i's risk aversion function. This means that R is a sort of harmonic mean of individual investors' risk aversion.

Another interpretation of R, the significance of which will be emphasized in later chapters, is as a *market price for risk* in the following sense. Suppose we consider all pairs of values of μ_j and b_j such that company value is the same. Then R is equal to the rate of substitution between μ_j and b_j for any firm, i.e.,

$$R = \frac{d\mu_j}{db_j}.$$

In other words, R measures the increase in expected return required to offset a unit's increase in the company's risk measure. It is in this sense that it will be natural for a firm that can exercise some discretion in determining μ_j and b_j to regard R as a "price of risk," and, as should be the case in competitive equilibrium, it is the same for all firms.

It is finally of interest to observe that, because of the dependence of R on the c_i, the introduction of additional investors, even if each possesses a very small amount of wealth, may substantially influence company values. The explanation of this nonintuitive result is quite simple. Even though an investor may have an insignificant amount of wealth, he may be able to borrow extensively, and in this way affect security demand on roughly the same scale as a wealthy investor.

4.11.   To illustrate the equilibrium solution, we shall give a numerical example involving two firms and two investors. The firms will be the same as those used in the examples in Chapter III; thus the means and covariances of returns are

$$\mu_1 = 1/2 \qquad \mu_2 = 5/4$$
$$\sigma_{11} = 1/4 \qquad \sigma_{12} = 1/8$$
$$\sigma_{21} = 1/8 \qquad \sigma_{22} = 3/16$$

From these data we get he risk measures for the companies as

$$b_1 = 3/8, \qquad b_2 = 5/16.$$

Further, let the coefficients of the investors' utility functions be $c_1 = 1/5$, $c_2 = 1/6$; hence $\sum_i 1/2c_i = 11/2$. Total expected return is $\sum_k \mu_k = 7/4$, so that the value of the market risk aversion factor is $R = 4/15$. Let the interest rate be zero (i.e., $r = 1$); the market valuation formula then gives the values of the two companies as

$$p_1 = 2/5, \qquad p_2 = 7/6.$$

Assume finally that the initial allocation is such that Investor 1 owns Company 1 and Investor 2 owns Company 2 and that neither company has any debt outstanding. Then initial wealths are clearly

$$W_1 = 2/5, \qquad W_2 = 7/6.$$

We can now find the corresponding optimal portfolios either by solving the equation system (5) for each investor, or, more simply, by using relation (7). Taking the latter approach, we find

$$\frac{1}{2c_1} - rW_1 = \frac{21}{10}$$

$$\frac{1}{2c_2} - rW_2 = \frac{11}{6}$$

so that $\sum_i 1/2c_i - r \sum_i W_i = 118/30$; from this we obtain

$$z_{11} = z_{12} = z_1 = \tfrac{63}{118}$$
$$z_{21} = z_{22} = z_2 = \tfrac{55}{118}.$$

The cost to Investor 1 of his investments in stocks is then $p_1 z_{11} + p_2 z_{12} = (p_1 + p_2)z_1 = 987/1180$; from his budget condition we then find his net lending as $m_1 = -103/236$, i.e., actually a borrowing. In the same way we find, as indeed we should, $m_2 = 103/236$. The resulting allocation in the three states of world are then given as follows (in units of 1/236):

TABLE 2

θ	Initial Allocation		Market Allocation	
	Inv. 1	Inv. 2	Inv. 1	Inv. 2
1	0	236	23	213
2	236	236	149	323
3	236	472	275	433

Some computation shows that the new allocation represents an increase in the expected utility of both investors; the trading is, as we would expect, to their mutual benefit.

4.12. By the *risk margin* of company value we mean the ratio between its expected rate of return, μ_j/v_j, and the riskless interest rate r. Thus, the risk margin is given by $\mu_j/rv_j = \mu_j/(\mu_j - Rb_j)$ and is thus independent of the numerical value of the interest rate. Thus, if the expected rate of return is 1.25 when $r = 1$ (as in the numerical example), if instead we had $r = 1.2$ it would be $1.25(1.2) = 1.50$. In the same way we see that the ratio between the expected rates of return of any two companies is also independent of the interest rate.

4.13. The results obtained above were based on the assumption that the preferences of all investors could be described by quadratic utility functions. From our earlier discussion of portfolio efficiency it should be evident that this assumption need not be explicit, since any efficient portfolio is one which maximizes the expectation of some quadratic utility function. Hence all that is needed is the assumption that investors select efficient portfolios; on several accounts this represents a weakening of the assumption of quadratic utility functions. We shall briefly restate the model in terms of mean-variance efficiency.

The mean and variance of investor i's portfolio return are

$$E_i = rW_i + \sum_j z_{ij}(\mu_j - rv_j)$$

$$S_i^2 = \sum_j \sum_k z_{ij} z_{ik} \sigma_{jk}.$$

To find the portfolio which minimizes S_i^2 for any given level of E_i, we form the Lagrangean

$$L_i = \sum_j \sum_k z_{ij} z_{ik} \sigma_{jk} + \lambda_i[E_i - rW_i - \sum_j z_{ij}(\mu_j - rv_j)]$$

and set the partial derivatives equal to zero:

$$\frac{\partial L_i}{\partial z_{ij}} = 2 \sum_k z_{ik} \sigma_{jk} - \lambda_i(\mu_j - rv_j) = 0$$

or

(10)
$$\sum_k \sigma_{jk} z_{ik} = \frac{\lambda_i}{2}(\mu_j - rv_j). \qquad \text{(all } i, j)$$

Now let z'_k be the solution of the system $\sum_k \sigma_{jk} z_k = \mu_j - rv_j$ (again assuming nonsingularity of the covariance matrix); the solution of (10) is then

$$z_{ik} = \frac{\lambda_i}{2} z'_k.$$

Summing over i and using the market clearing conditions we obtain

$$\sum_i z_{ik} = \tfrac{1}{2} z'_k \sum_i \lambda_i = 1,$$

giving

$$z'_k = \frac{2}{\sum_i \lambda_i}$$

and hence

$$z_{ik} = \frac{\lambda_i}{\sum_i \lambda_i}$$

where the RHS is again independent of k. Hence $z_{ik} = z_i$ for all k. With this solution substituted in (10) we can solve for v_j as

$$v_j = \frac{1}{r}\left(\mu_j - \frac{2}{\sum_i \lambda_i} b_j\right),$$

where b_j is defined as before. It is clear that in this formulation the factor $2/\sum_i \lambda_i$ corresponds to (and must indeed be identical with) the market risk aversion factor R of the quadratic model. We know from the theory of Lagrange multipliers that λ_i represents the marginal rate of substitution between the variance and the mean of the portfolio return, i.e., $\lambda_i = dS_i^2/dE_i$; hence the smaller λ_i, the stronger the investor's risk aversion. This immediately allows $2/\sum_i \lambda_i$ to be interpreted as a market risk aversion index. Hence all the properties of the quadratic model carry over to the "efficiency model."

4.14. The reason why we can consider the efficiency model as representing an important generalization of the quadratic model has already been indicated in Chapter III. We referred there to evidence that the return distributions for well diversified portfolios can be very accurately approximated by two-parameter distributions. Further, we would expect any reasonable set of preferences to lead to a fairly well diversified portfolio. Therefore, regardless of investors' utility functions, they will select portfolios which are, for all practical purposes, efficient. This in turn means that the principal properties of the model are, for all practical purposes, independent of any assumptions about investors' preferences.

The argument of the preceding paragraph is a very important step in the derivation of an operational theory of share valuation and financial decision making, and should be kept clearly in mind. We argue, in effect, that an assumption that investors select efficient portfolios serves the purpose of simplifying the derivation of such a theory, but that the generality of our results is not significantly affected by this assumption.

4.15. One important characteristic of the market valuation model is that the total value of the company, v_j, does not depend on its level of debt, d_j. This result confirms the well known Proposition I of Modigliani and Miller [2]: the total value of the firm depends only on the probability distribution for gross yield (as represented by μ_j and b_j), not on its capital structure. Thus, if d_j is increased by a given amount without any change in the probability distribution for X_j, then the value of shares falls by precisely the same amount. This conclusion was to be anticipated from the observation that the probability distributions for the Y_i depend on the v_j only. This fact holds regardless of what assumptions we make about investor preferences or probability estimates. In Chapter V we shall show that the proposition indeed holds under extremely general conditions, but at this point we shall only attempt to clarify the idea behind the result by considering a simple numerical example.

If a change in the amount of debt causes the equity value to change by the same amount in the opposite direction, the value of the investor's share holdings, and so also his bond holdings, will change. The important point, however, is that he is able to replicate the probability distribution for final wealth by such a change in his personal leverage. To see this, suppose a company has a gross return of either $X(1) = 1400$ or $X(2) = 1700$ in two states of the world. Let the interest rate be 5 per cent, and assume that in the first situation the value of the firm is $v = 1500$, consisting of equity value $p = 1000$ and debt $d = 500$. Return to equity is thus $R(1) = 1400 - 1.05(500) = 875$ and $R(2) = 1700 - 1.05(500) = 1175$ in the two states. Assume further that there are two investors with amounts of wealth $W_1 = 1000$ and $W_2 = 700$, and that in the initial situation they own the fractions $z_1 = 0.6$ and $z_2 = 0.4$ of the company; their bond holdings are then $m_1 = 1000 - 0.6(1000) = 400$ and $m_2 = 700 - 0.4(1000) = 300$. Their final wealth (exclusive of ownership in other companies) in the two states of the world are thus

$$Y_1(1) = 1.05(400) + 0.6(875) = 945$$
$$Y_1(2) = 1.05(400) + 0.6(1175) = 1125$$

and

$$Y_2(1) = 1.05(300) + 0.4(875) = 665$$
$$Y_2(2) = 1.05(300) + 0.4(1175) = 785.$$

Consider now the second situation, in which the company has zero debt, but its gross return and total value are as before. Suppose further that investors make no changes in the proportions owned of the company, but adjust their lending to accomodate the change in share value. Thus, $m_1 = 1000 - 0.6(1500) = 100$ and $m_2 = 700 - 0.4(1500) = 100$. Their final wealth in the two states are therefore

$$Y_1(1) = 1.05(100) + 0.6(1400) = 945$$
$$Y_1(2) = 1.05(100) + 0.6(1700) = 1125$$

and

$$Y_2(1) = 1.05(100) + 0.4(1400) = 665$$
$$Y_2(2) = 1.05(100) + 0.4(1700) = 785$$

which are precisely the same as in the first situation. Hence, if investors obtained their preferred return distributions in the first situation, they have no reason to change their demand for shares; as a consequence, the market for shares as well as bonds will clear and cause no change in total company values.

Although the proposition is of rather general validity, it should be emphasized that it is concerned *only* with company value under alternative levels of debt, other things being equal. In particular, the economic activity of the company as represented by its gross return X_j is assumed to be the same. This means that if we were to plot v_j against d_j for different firms, we would not expect the plot to be along a horizontal line, one obvious reason being that larger firms tend (for some reason) to have more debt. If a dependence exists between the funds raised by borrowing and the level of operations carried out by the firms, then a corresponding dependence would be observed between debt level and market value. It is probably true that some of the controversy over the Modigliani–Miller proposition was the result of misunderstanding of its *ceteris paribus* nature.

To an economist, the irrelevance of the debt level perhaps seems self-evident. Subdivision of company value is after all nothing but a way of channeling ownership or claims to income streams two different ways. The value of the company should depend on the total income stream, and not on how it is channeled to the market.

4.16.   One interesting application of the market valuation model is to consider the effect of a reorganization of economic activity among firms. Suppose the economy consists of three companies (1, 2, 3), and that companies 2 and 3 are merged so as to form a new company which we shall label a. Suppose furthermore that the return of the merged company is just equal to the sum of the returns of the old companies:

$$X_a = X_2 + X_3;$$

this means that no net gains through economies of scale are realized by the merger. It is then clear that the expected return of the new company is

$$\mu_a = \mu_2 + \mu_3,$$

and as for the new covariance terms we find

$$\sigma_{1a} = \sigma_{a1} = \mathcal{E}[(X_1 - \mu_1)(X_a - \mu_a)] = \sigma_{12} + \sigma_{13}$$
$$\sigma_{aa} = \mathcal{E}[(X_a - \mu_a)^2] = \sigma_{22} + 2\sigma_{23} + \sigma_{33}.$$

This means that the risk measure of the new company is

$$\begin{aligned}
b_a = \sigma_{1a} + \sigma_{aa} &= (\sigma_{12} + \sigma_{13}) + (\sigma_{22} + 2\sigma_{23} + \sigma_{33}) \\
&= (\sigma_{21} + \sigma_{22} + \sigma_{23}) + (\sigma_{31} + \sigma_{32} + \sigma_{33}) \\
&= b_2 + b_3.
\end{aligned}$$

It then follows that

$$v_a = \frac{1}{r}[(\mu_2 + \mu_3) + R(b_2 + b_3)] = v_2 + v_3;$$

the value of the new company is just equal to the sum of the values of the old companies. It is then easy to see that by continuing to hold the same percentage in the new company as they held in the old companies, investors will maintain identical probability distributions for portfolio return. In short, everything remains essentially the same as before the merger. Investors will accept the exchange of securities caused by the reorganization of companies, but will undertake no further adjustments.

The meaning of this result is clearly that the organization of productive activities is immaterial from the standpoint of valuation. Accordingly, companies may be formed in the way most efficient for carrying out the productive activities (given such phenomena as economies of scale), and that organization will also prove adequate from a financial markets point of view.

This conclusion may seem to be at variance with the recent conglomerate merger fad. In their extreme form, conglomerate mergers involve firms whose activities are unrelated, and consequently economies of scale are largely absent. From a stockholder point of view there would seem to be nothing to be gained from such a merger. Curiously enough, the principal explanation of (or defense for) conglomerate mergers is that they allow firms to diversify and thus spread out risk. However, with an efficient security market there is no need for an individual company to diversify, since stockholders can obtain precisely the same effect by diversifying their own portfolios (which is just what they do if they act rationally). Dismaying as the idea may seem to a particular company's board of directors, the market doesn't give a damn for the legal entity called the company; it is the real side of the economy that matters, not how ownership is organized.

4.17. Market indifference to ownership arrangements is explained in part by the high degree of portfolio diversification implied by our model. As noted earlier, the hypothesis that an investor owns the same fraction of shares in all companies ($z_{ij} = z_i$ for all j) often seems violated in practice. We shall enumerate some of the more important reasons for these discrepancies.

One obvious reason for holding unbalanced portfolios is the existence of transactions cost, which our model has not taken into account. By transactions cost we mean not only such direct costs as brokerage fees, but, perhaps more importantly, the opportunity cost of collecting information and reviewing and revising portfolio positions. For small personal investors these costs may be relatively high, leading to concentration in a very few securities. The availability of investment indirectly through mutual funds may make transactions costs less important for the personal investor.

Perhaps one of the most important reasons for departure from a perfectly balanced portfolio is the presence of strong stochastic dependence among certain securities. This would mean that a number of securities can be considered as near-perfect substitutes for each other, in which case one stock may be chosen as representative of the whole group. Thus, if I think all aluminum shares will move very closely together, I need not buy shares in each individual company, but rather invest in one representative firm. I should then invest an amount proportional to the outstanding shares of the industry as a whole. The possibility that one stock may serve as a representative of a larger group in no way invalidates the market valuation formula (9). As we shall see, the existence of such "risk homogeneous" classes of stocks may explain a large part of the discrepancies between real world and balanced portfolios.

Portfolio decisions may be based on "irrational" criteria, by which we do not mean senseless, but rather that factors other than the probability distribution for return are taken into account. Making a killing in the stock market may provide conversational value or enhance the investor's reputation for shrewdness, which may have value quite independent of the monetary gains involved. It should be kept in mind that (apart from using inside information) the only way to get ahead of the crowd in the stock market is to make an ex ante foolish decision, such as putting all your funds in a single stock. Unfortunately, this is also the way to get behind the crowd, but there, at least, nobody may notice you. Such extrapecuniary motives may be particularly prevalent in institutional investment activity, where an account manager may be more interested in attracting his superiors' attention to his cleverness than in providing a dull, but sensibly balanced, portfolio for the client.

The investor may have nonportfolio income which is correlated with certain securities. If I am an architect, my professional income may be closely correlated with earnings in the construction and building materials industries. A rational portfolio would in this case include relatively fewer shares in these industries.

A frequently cited reason for the holding of unbalanced portfolios is that investors do not, contrary to the assumption of our model, hold identical beliefs about the probability distributions for company yields. While this is obviously correct in itself, it is somewhat more difficult to see how the existence of heterogeneous beliefs would affect the empirical validity of the market valuation formula (9). We shall examine this in more detail in the following chapter.

4.18. Although there may be various reasons for an individual investor to depart from a balanced portfolio, it is less clear why a mutual fund should do so. Of course, all mutual funds are highly diversified, but they nevertheless appear to be, or claim to be, differentiated by their investment policy; some funds hold relatively more speculative and "growth" stocks ("growth stock" funds) than others ("balanced" funds).

In discussing mutual funds, it should be kept in mind that, from a financial markets point of view, mutual funds are just instruments for owning shares in ordinary companies indirectly. Hence the only independent value (share value above value of assets) can come from the fund's superior efficiency in managing large portfolios. In the absence of transactions costs, the market value of the mutual fund could be no higher than the market value of its security holdings. Suppose there were two companies with market values of p_1 and p_2, and that there was a mutual fund with share value p_0 owning 20 per cent of Company 1 and 40 per cent of Company 2. Suppose further that I as an investor find it optimal to hold 10 per cent in each of the two companies. If I acquire the shares directly, the cost will be $.1(p_1 + p_2)$. However, I can also effect the same holdings indirectly by buying a 25 per cent interest in the mutual fund and supplementing this with a 5 per cent direct holding in Company 1. The cost of such an arrangement would be $.25p_0 + .05p_1$. If there are no transactions costs, the value of the holdings under the two arrangements must be the same, since they give rise to identical return patterns. But setting $.1(p_1 + p_2) = .25p_0 + .05p_1$ gives $p_0 = .2p_1 + .4p_2$, where the RHS is simply the market value of the fund's assets.

We might then ask: If individual investors prefer to hold equal proportions of the stock of all companies, why should not mutual funds also do so, and thus save investors the trouble of supplementing their holdings on the outside? The usual explanation of the existence of funds with different share composition is that they appeal to different *clienteles*. Precisely what distinguishes different clienteles is not so clear, however. If we look at the above discussion of factors that may cause individual portfolios to be incompletely balanced, it is hard to see how any of these could cause a systematic clientele effect. Take, for example, the case of correlation with nonportfolio income. We could conceivably organize an Architect's Mutual Fund with relatively small holdings in the construction and building materials industries and thus attract a certain clientele, but such arrangements do not seem to be of any practical importance. Existence of differing probability estimates might make possible a certain clientele appeal, but this would be of a more accidental nature. For example, a mutual fund might invest relatively heavily in certain firms or industries, and thereby attract investors who happened to think that the shares of precisely those firms or industries were undervalued. Whether such beliefs are related to other characteristics of the investor is rather questionable.

The idea of a clientele effect is popularly associated with such variables as stage in life cycle, attitude to risk, amount of wealth, and relative security of nonportfolio income. Thus, widows and orphans would prefer a "balanced" fund, while the young and aggressive, or the tenured professor, would be more interested in a speculative fund. However, on the basis of our model, we have to reject such ideas. A difference in risk aversion does not in itself induce different asset proportions; as we have seen, only the *size* of the risky part of the portfolio is affected.

Whether mutual funds with differently stated objectives do or do not compose their risky portfolios differently is of course an empirical question, but no systematic empirical analysis seems to be available. To throw some light on the question, we shall examine some rough data on two mutual funds under the same management—the balanced fund and the stock fund of Eaton & Howard as of May 1, 1969.[1] Since both funds are run by the same management, the estimates of the relevant yield characteristics of stocks should be quite homogeneous.

The first important observation was that the relative sizes of riskless or near-riskless and risky parts of the total portfolios were quite different: the balanced fund had 35.5 per cent of its assets in bonds, preferred stock, government notes, and cash, while the stock fund had only 8.5 per cent of its assets in those types of investments. This would clearly explain a large portion of the difference in overall riskiness of the funds.

The remaining, risky assets held by the stock fund had a value of approximately 2.2 times that of the risky assets held by the balanced fund. It was then natural to test whether this value ratio was the same for all shares held by the two funds. Some quick calculations showed this to be far from true: the ratio varied from .27 (General Public Utilities) to 4.02 (Eastman Kodak).

Since the funds did not hold all the same stocks, a comparison was also made by 20-industry classification. The range here was also considerable: from .45 (electric utilities) to 6.46 (photography).

However, by grouping together three or fewer industries with correlation coefficients of approximately .9 or higher (based on Farrar's data [1]), a quite different picture emerges (see Table 3). As indicated, each group consists of industries with closely correlated returns, and we observe that the pattern of investment over groups is strikingly similar for the two funds. Thus, although there are obvious inconsistencies on the level of individual stocks or industries, when these are aggregated into risk-homogeneous industry groups the data do not seem inconsistent with the hypothesis that both funds differ mainly with respect to the size of their risky portfolios.

4.19.   It is a popular notion in certain circles that without inside information, portfolio selection might just as well be made on a random basis. It may be of some interest to examine such a proposition in the light of our market model. Since it is not always clear precisely on what basis the proposition is made, we shall consider two possible lines of argument.

One interpretation is based on the idea that when share prices are in equilibrium, they will properly reflect all relevant return characteristics of the

[1] I gratefully acknowledge the assistance of David H. Smith in collecting and preparing the data.

TABLE 3

Value of Stock Held in Industry Groups, in Thousands of Dollars

Industry Group	Balanced Fund	Stock Fund	Ratio
Banking, Electronics-Aerospace, Household products	23,754	51,906	2.18
Photography, Oil, Retail trade	30,839	68,916	2.23
Insurance, Building	13,788	31,613	2.29
Metals and mining, Industrial equipment, Automotive	12,182	26,285	2.16
Industrial products, Business services, Consumer goods	15,945	35,549	2.22

stock; hence, there will be no obvious "good buys" available. If it is felt that railroads are in for trouble, railroad shares will be correspondingly low. Thus, it may be argued, since you get what you pay for, it does not make any difference what you buy.

There is an obvious flaw in such an argument. Consider, as an analogy, a housing market which is in equilibrium in the sense that the prevailing prices reflect all relevant characteristics of each house: its style and physical properties, the view, closeness to schools and shopping, the character of the neighborhood, and so on. This certainly does not mean that I am personally indifferent among all houses, and would be willing to buy one at random. Market prices reflect preferences with respect to various characteristics in an *average* sense, whereas my personal preferences may be different from this average. In the same way, share prices reflect yield characteristics as evaluated by investors on the average, whereas my personal preferences determine a portfolio which is optimal specifically for me.

Another line of argument is closely related to the idea (and considerable empirical evidence) that data based on past history of stock prices have little or no relevance for predicting future stock price behavior. If this evidence is accepted, a portfolio chosen at random may perform just as well as one which is efficient, but relative only to what is basically equivalent to a randomly chosen set of means and covariances. This argument is not really concerned with the optimality of random portfolio selection at all, but rather with the irrelevance of past performance for portfolio selection purposes. We conclude, then, that the arguments for random portfolio selection appear shaky or misdirected at best.

4.20. It is of some interest to compare the market valuation formula (9) with that of Modigliani and Miller [2]. In their formulation, company value is given by

$$(11) \qquad\qquad\qquad v_j = \frac{\mu_j}{\rho_j}$$

where ρ_j is the company's "cost of capital." We shall discuss the concept of cost of capital in more detail in Chapter VII, and here only note the relationship between the two formulae.

If the two expressions for market value are to be consistent with each other, we must clearly have

$$\frac{\mu_j}{\rho_j} = \frac{1}{r}(\mu_j - Rb_j).$$

Solving for ρ_j, we obtain

$$\rho_j = \frac{r}{1 - Rb_j/\mu_j}.$$

Thus, unless b_j is negative, ρ_j is larger than the riskless interest rate—more so the larger the risk measure b_j, less so the larger the expected gross yield μ_j.

Modigliani and Miller's cost of capital concept has a special significance in relation to their risk class assumption, described as follows:

> We shall assume that firms can be divided into "equivalent return" classes such that the return on shares issued by any firm in any given class is proportional to (and hence perfectly correlated with) the return on the shares issued by any other firm in the same class. This assumption implies that the various shares within the same class differ, at most, by a "scale factor."[2]

Even though they use the expression "return on shares," it is clear from the subsequent analysis that the assumption refers to gross return, not necessarily the return on equity. The assumption, therefore, is that firms can be divided into risk classes such that two firms, j and k, belong to the same class if, and only if,

$$X_k = \alpha X_j.$$

It is now easy to see that with this assumption we have

$$\mu_k = \alpha\mu_j, \qquad b_k = \alpha b_j$$

[2]F. Modigliani and M. H. Miller, "The Cost of Capital, Corporation Finance, and the Theory of Investment," *American Economic Review*, 1958, p. 266.

and consequently that $b_k/\mu_k = b_j/\mu_j$. This is then seen to imply that the cost of capital, whatever it is, is equal for the two firms.

REFERENCES

1. Farrar, D. E. *The Investment Decision Under Uncertainty.* Englewood Cliffs, N.J.: Prentice-Hall, Inc., 1962.
2. Modigliani, F., and M. H. Miller. "The Cost of Capital, Corporation Finance, and the Theory of Investment," *Amer. Econ. Rev.*, 1958, pp. 261–297.
3. Mossin, J. "Equilibrium in a Capital Asset Market," *Econometrica*, 1966, pp. 768–783.
4. ———. "Security Pricing and Investment Criteria in Competitive Markets," *Amer. Econ. Rev.*, 1969, pp. 749–756.
5. Sharpe, W. F. "Capital Asset Prices: A Theory of Market Equilibrium under Conditions of Risk," *Jour. Finance*, 1964, pp. 425–442.

5 Extensions

of the Valuation Model

5.1. The market valuation model developed in the preceding chapter rests on a number of assumptions with respect to both investors' beliefs and preferences and the economic opportunities available to them. Some of these assumptions have already been discussed. In particular, we argued that the assumption that investors choose mean-variance efficient portfolios probably was much less restrictive than it might appear at first glance.

In this chapter we shall consider some further assumptions which appear to be crucial, and see how our conclusions must be modified if these assumptions are relaxed. These are treated in a separate chapter because the analysis becomes somewhat technical at times, and some readers may want to skip or skim it. They should be able to do so without serious loss of continuity.

5.2. We shall be concerned primarily with two aspects of the theory: the Modigliani-Miller Proposition I (MMI) on the irrelevance of debt level for valuation, and the validity of the market valuation formula derived in Chapter IV. We know that when the market valuation formula is valid, the MMI also holds, but the MMI is clearly a weaker proposition than the market valuation formula and may therefore hold under less restrictive assumptions. We shall show that this indeed is the case.

We shall be interested in examining the effect on these propositions of modifying our earlier assumptions in the following ways:

1. To allow completely arbitrary investor preferences (i.e., preferences which do not necessarily imply mean-variance efficient portfolios);
2. To allow heterogeneous beliefs;
3. To allow the possibility of default on corporate debt so that corporate bonds are no longer riskless securities with fixed interest payments;
4. To allow lending rates to be stochastic and possibly different for different investors.

5.3. By default risk we shall simply mean that for some or all companies there is a positive probability that gross return will be insufficient for servicing its debt, in which case bondholders receive whatever is available, while shareholders receive nothing. This obviously means that bonds are no longer riskless securities; the bonds of different companies are no longer perfect substitutes for each other, and we have to distinguish among an investor's bond holdings in different companies. Furthermore, the *contractual interest rate* on a company's bonds, i.e., the rate it will have to pay if it does not go bankrupt, will now be determined by the market in the same way as share prices. We shall denote (one plus) the contractual interest rate for company j by r_j.

The amount required to service company j's debt is $r_j d_j$, but the amount actually received by bondholders is now a random variable B_j with a distribution described by

$$B_j = \begin{cases} r_j d_j & \text{if } X_j > r_j d_j \\ X_j & \text{otherwise.} \end{cases}$$

Clearly, the payment to shareholders is just $R_j = X_j - B_j$, i.e.,

$$R_j = \begin{cases} X_j - r_j d_j & \text{if } X_j > r_j d_j \\ 0 & \text{otherwise.} \end{cases}$$

5.4. We shall start by showing that *the MMI holds under all of the conditions listed in section 5.2.* To do so, we shall first prove a somewhat more general proposition, and then show that the MMI follows from it. This proposition, which we may refer to as the *additivity proposition*, can be stated as follows:

> *In equilibrium, the market value of the sum of the returns on a set of securities is equal to the sum of the market values of the returns on those securities.*

This proposition clearly represents a generalization of our earlier analysis of the effect of mergers on market valuation. It is easily proved by a formal inspection of the equations defining equilibrium.

Assume that in the "initial" situation there are n securities with returns X_j ($j = 1, \ldots, n$) and m investors facing the possibly random lending rates Q_i ($i = 1, \ldots, m$). Let the market value of the jth security be v_j; the equations defining equilibrium under our new assumptions are then given by

$$\text{(1a)} \qquad \mathcal{E}_i[u_i'(Y_i)(X_j - Q_i v_j)] = 0 \qquad (j = 1, \ldots, n;\ i = 1, \ldots, m)$$

$$\text{(1b)} \qquad \sum_i z_{ij} = 1 \qquad (j = 1, \ldots, n).$$

These equations correspond to equations (3) and (4) of Chapter IV. The difference is that a subscript i has been added to the expectation operator to allow heterogeneous beliefs, and that the riskless interest rate r has been replaced by the random lending rates Q_i. Furthermore, the specifications of the utility functions are completely arbitrary.

Assume now (without loss of generality) that the return on the first k securities were combined to form the return $X_a = \sum_{j=1}^k X_j$. Let the market value of X_a be v_a. The equations defining equilibrium in this situation would be

$$\text{(2a)} \qquad \begin{cases} \mathcal{E}_i[u_i'(Y_i)(X_a - Q_i v_a)] = 0 \\ \mathcal{E}_i[u_i'(Y_i)(X_j - Q_i v_j)] = 0 \qquad (j = k+1, \ldots, n) \end{cases} \Big\}\ (i = 1, \ldots, m)$$

$$\text{(2b)} \qquad \begin{cases} \sum_i z_{ia} = 1 \\ \sum_i z_{ij} = 1 \qquad (j = k+1, \ldots, n). \end{cases}$$

The problem now is to show that if $v_1, \ldots, v_n$ is a solution to (1), and $v_a, v_{k+1}', \ldots, v_n'$ a solution to (2), then

$$\text{(3)} \qquad v_a = \sum_{j=1}^k v_j,\ v_{k+1}', = v_{k+1}, \ldots, v_n' = v_n.$$

But this is quite easily shown to be true, for it is clear, through summation of the first k equations of (1a) and (1b), that (1a) and (1b) imply

$$\text{(4a)} \qquad \begin{cases} \mathcal{E}_i\left[u_i'(Y_i)\left(X_a - Q_i \sum_{j=1}^k v_j\right)\right] = 0 \\ \mathcal{E}_i[u_i'(Y_i)(X_j - Q_i v_j)] = 0 \qquad (j = k+1, \ldots, n) \end{cases} \Big\}\ (i = 1, \ldots, m)$$

$$\text{(4b)} \qquad \begin{cases} \sum_i \left(\frac{1}{k} \sum_{j=1}^k z_{ij}\right) = 1 \\ \sum_i z_{ij} = 1 \qquad (j = k+1, \ldots, n). \end{cases}$$

These equations are identical with (2) except that v_a has been replaced by

$$\sum_{j=1}^{k} v_j \quad \text{and} \quad z_{ia} \text{ by } \frac{1}{k}\sum_{j=1}^{k} z_{ij}.$$

It then follows immediately that (3) must hold; hence the additivity proposition has been established.

5.5. The additivity proposition was stated without explicit reference to the possibility of default risk. However, it is now easy to see that, as stated, the additivity proposition implies that the MMI holds in the presence of default risk. There is nothing in the proof of the additivity proposition which prevents us from interpreting two of the returns on the given securities as the return on the shares alone and the return on the bonds alone of the same company. That is, we can take, say, X_1 to be the return to shareholders and X_2 the return to bondholders in the same company a, and v_1 and v_2 as the market values of the shares and bonds, respectively. By assumption, the sum of the *returns* is given independently of the amount of debt and is equal to the gross return X_a of the company. But then it follows from the additivity proposition that the sum of the *values* of the two securities, $v_1 + v_2 = v_a$, is also independent of the amount of debt, which is precisely the MMI.

We have thus established that the MMI holds under very general conditions. The result indicates that, apart from taxes, the only factor of practical interest that might affect the proposition's validity would be market imperfections, such as certain forms of transactions costs. It is extremely difficult to incorporate such imperfections in a formal analysis, however, and we shall not pursue the problem further.

5.6. We now turn to an examination of the validity of the market valuation formula under less restrictive assumptions than those made in Chapter IV. Here, however, we have to proceed somewhat more carefully, and shall analyze only one assumption at a time, retaining the others as before. Thus we shall start with allowing the presence of default risk, while still assuming mean-variance efficiency, homogeneous beliefs, and that investors can, apart from corporate bond holdings, lend and borrow at a riskless rate if they so choose.

It is perhaps obvious that, under these assumptions, the market valuation formula will continue to hold. Suppose the company had no debt; then there would not be any default chances either, in which case we would be back to the model of Chapter IV, with company value given by $v_j = (\mu_j - Rb_j)/r$. But we have now shown that the market value is independent of debt level when there is default risk. Therefore, the introduction of debt (and default risk) does not affect the value of v_j, hence the market valuation formula remains valid.

It is possible to establish the validity of the market valuation formula under default risk more directly by formulating a general equilibrium model which explicitly includes investors' demand for the bonds of different companies, and then showing that the market valuation formula can be derived from it. To do so we have, as already pointed out, to distinguish among an investor's bond holdings in different companies, since they are no longer perfect substitutes for each other. Thus, we introduce y_{ij} as the fraction owned of company j's outstanding bonds. Then, letting z_{ij} be the fraction owned of outstanding shares, we can write investor i's budget equation as

$$W_i = m_i + \sum_j (y_{ij}d_j + z_{ij}p_j)$$

where m_i, as before, is his net lending at the riskless rate. Final wealth is now given by

$$Y_i = rm_i + \sum_j (y_{ij}B_j + z_{ij}R_j),$$

where B_j and R_j are as defined in section 5.3. When m_i is substituted in the budget equation, Y_i can be written as

$$Y_i = rW_i + \sum_j [y_{ij}(B_j - rd_j) + z_{ij}(R_j - rp_j)].$$

Expected final wealth is

$$E_i = rW_i + \sum_j [y_{ij}(\bar{B}_j - rd_j) + z_{ij}(\bar{R}_j - rp_j)],$$

where $\bar{B}_j = \mathcal{E}(B_j)$ and $\bar{R}_j = \mathcal{E}(R_j)$. With this we have

$$Y_i - E_i = \sum_j [y_{ij}(B_j - \bar{B}_j) + z_{ij}(R_j - \bar{R}_j)]$$

and thus

$$\begin{aligned}(Y_i - E_i)^2 = \sum_j \sum_k [&y_{ij}y_{ik}(B_j - \bar{B}_j)(B_k - \bar{B}_k) \\ &+ 2y_{ij}z_{ik}(B_j - \bar{B}_j)(R_k - \bar{R}_k) \\ &+ z_{ij}z_{ik}(R_j - \bar{R}_j)(R_k - \bar{R}_k)],\end{aligned}$$

hence the variance $V_i = \mathcal{E}(Y_i - E_i)^2$ is given by

$$\begin{aligned}V_i = \sum_j \sum_k [&y_{ij}y_{ik} \operatorname{Cov}(B_j, B_k) + 2y_{ij}z_{ik} \operatorname{Cov}(B_j, R_k) \\ &+ z_{ij}z_{ik} \operatorname{Cov}(R_j, R_k)].\end{aligned}$$

To find the efficient portfolios, i.e., those which minimize V_i for any given value of E_i, we proceed as before by forming the Lagrangean

$$L_i = V_i + \lambda_i \{ E_i - rW_i - \sum_j [y_{ij}(\bar{B} - rd_j) + z_{ij}(\bar{R}_j - rp_j)] \}$$

and set the partial derivatives with respect to both the y_{ij} and the z_{ij} equal to zero:

(5a) $\dfrac{\partial L_i}{\partial y_{ij}} = 2 \sum_k [y_{ik} \, \mathrm{Cov}\,(B_j, B_k) + z_{ik} \, \mathrm{Cov}\,(B_j, R_k)] - \lambda_i(\bar{B}_j - rd_j) = 0$

$$(j = 1, \ldots, n)$$

(5b) $\dfrac{\partial L_i}{\partial z_{ij}} = 2 \sum_k [y_{ik} \, \mathrm{Cov}\,(B_j, R_k) + z_{ik} \, \mathrm{Cov}\,(R_j, R_k)] - \lambda_i(\bar{R}_j - rp_j) = 0$

$$(j = 1, \ldots, n),$$

Because of the constant factor λ_i in all equations, we must clearly have

$$\frac{y_{ij}}{\lambda_i} = \frac{y_{1j}}{\lambda_1}$$

for all i; hence

$$\sum_i y_{ij} = \frac{y_{1j}}{\lambda_1} \sum_i \lambda_i$$

which by the market clearing conditions must equal unity. Therefore,

$$\frac{y_{1j}}{\lambda_1} = \frac{1}{\sum\limits_i \lambda_i}$$

and hence in general

$$y_{ij} = \frac{\lambda_i}{\sum\limits_i \lambda_i}.$$

It is easy to see that precisely the same relations must hold for the z_{ij}; this means that for all j we have

$$y_{ij} = z_{ij} = \frac{\lambda_i}{\sum\limits_i \lambda_i}.$$

That is, any investor holds the same percentage of both the stocks and the bonds of every company.

Equations (5a) and (5b) can now be written

$$2 \sum_k [\text{Cov}(B_j, B_k) + \text{Cov}(B_j, R_k)] = (\bar{B}_j - rd_j) \sum_i \lambda_i$$

$$2 \sum_k [\text{Cov}(B_j, R_k) + \text{Cov}(R_j, R_k)] = (\bar{R}_j - rp_j) \sum_i \lambda_i$$

for all j. Adding together these two equations we obtain

(6) $$2 \sum_k [\text{Cov}(B_j, B_k) + 2 \text{Cov}(B_j, R_k) + \text{Cov}(R_j, R_k)]$$

$$= (\mu_j - rv_j) \sum_i \lambda_i$$

since $\bar{B}_j + \bar{R}_j = \mu_j$ and $d_j + p_j = v_j$. It is now easily verified that the expression in brackets on the LHS reduces to nothing but σ_{jk}, the covariance between X_j and X_k. The equations (6) then become

$$2 \sum_k \sigma_{jk} = (\mu_j - rv_j) \sum_i \lambda_i$$

which can be solved for v_j as

$$v_j = \frac{1}{r}(\mu_j - Rb_j)$$

where $R = 2/\sigma \lambda_i$ and $b_j = \sum_k \sigma_{jk}$ as before. We thus conclude that the market valuation formula is unaffected by the introduction of default risk.

5.7.   In the preceding analysis we did not explicitly consider the market determination of the contractual interest rate, r_j. Our formulation implied that r_j is determined so as to make the market value of the bonds equal to their face value. Strictly speaking, this is merely a convention; we could just as well have taken the contractual interest rate as being arbitrarily set and let the market determine a trading price not necessarily at par. As we shall see, however, it is analytically more satisfactory to fix the market value of the bonds at par, and let the market's evaluation of their return be reflected in the interest rate. We shall demonstrate how r_j can be determined in this way.

From the additivity proposition it follows that when the market valuation formula is valid, it can be used to calculate the values of shares and bonds separately on the basis of the probability distribution for their return. Now, to any particular value of r_j there will correspond a certain probability distribution for return to bondholders. On the basis of the market valuation formula, we can then calculate the corresponding market value of the bonds. By requiring this value to be equal to the given amount of debt outstanding, we can determine r_j.

It is difficult to derive the equilibrium value of r_j in a simple way for an arbitrary probability distribution for gross return. We shall therefore only illustrate the procedure for the case where the gross return has a two-point distribution independent of the returns of other firms. On intuitive grounds this simplification would not seem to affect seriously the general nature of our conclusions. Thus, we assume that X_j has a probability distribution of the form

X_j	$\Pr(X_j)$
β	p
α	$1 - p$

such that $\alpha > \beta$. We further assume the outcome α is large enough to guarantee against default at any "reasonable" interest rate, while β is so small that default will necessarily occur. For example, if the debt level is 1500 and $\alpha = 1200$, $\beta - 2400$, this condition is satisfied as long as the interest rate is less than 60 per cent. The corresponding probability distributions for return to bondholders, B_j, and shareholders, R_j, are then

B_j	$\Pr(B_j)$	R_j	$\Pr(R_j)$
β	p	0	p
$r_j d_j$	$1 - p$	$\alpha - r_j d_j$	$1 - p$

so that the means, variances, and covariance between B_j and R_j are given by

$$\bar{B}_j = (1 - p)r_j d_j + p\beta \qquad \bar{R}_j = (1 - p)(\alpha - r_j d_j)$$
$$\sigma_B^2 = p(1 - p)(r_j d_j - \beta)^2 \quad \sigma_R^2 = p(1 - p)(\alpha - r_j d_j)^2$$
$$\text{Cov}(B_j, R_j) = p(1 - p)[(\alpha + \beta)r_j d_j - r_j^2 d_j^2 - \alpha\beta].$$

Since we assume X_j to be uncorrelated with the return of other firms, the risk measure for the return to bondholders, b_B, is simply

$$b_B = \sigma_B^2 + \text{Cov}(B_j, R_j)$$
$$= p(1 - p)(\alpha - \beta)(r_j d_j - \beta),$$

so that the value of the bonds is given by

$$v_B = \frac{1}{r}(\bar{B} - Rb_B)$$

$$= \frac{1}{r}[(1 - p)r_j d_j + p\beta - Rp(1 - p)(\alpha - \beta)(r_j d_j - \beta)].$$

By now requiring $v_B = d_j$, we can solve for r_j as

(7)
$$r_j = (1 + a)r - a\frac{\beta}{d_j}$$

where

$$a = \frac{p[1 + R(1 - p)(\alpha - \beta)]}{(1 - p)[1 - Rp(\alpha - \beta)]}.$$

As a numerical example, suppose

$$\alpha = 2400$$
$$\beta = 1200$$
$$p = .1$$
$$R = 1/1080$$
$$r = 1.04$$

Then $a = .25$, and r_j is given by

$$r_j = 1.30 - \frac{300}{d_j},$$

giving the following contractual interest rates for different debt levels:

Amount of Debt	Interest Rate
1200	5%
1500	10%
1800	$13\frac{1}{3}$%

5.8.   The next assumption we shall examine is that a riskless asset exists. It may be argued that no such asset exists in the real world, since even assets like government bonds or savings deposits are subject to the vagaries of uncertain price level changes. Apart from changes in the price level, the lending rate, although riskless at any point in time, may change over the investor's horizon in an unpredictable way. We shall therefore see what happens when the lending rate is assumed to be uncertain. We shall still assume that the lending rate will be the same for all investors, however, so that its mean and covariances with the X_j are the same for all investors. For simplicity, we shall also assume that firms issue no debt.

We let Q denote the uncertain lending rate, and write its mean as $\bar{Q}$, the variance as σ_{qq}, and the covariances with the X_j as σ_{qj}. Then final wealth is given by

$$Y_i = W_i Q + \sum_j z_{ij}(X_j - p_j Q),$$

so that expected final wealth is

$$E_i = W_j \bar{Q} + \sum_j z_{ij}(\mu_j - p_j \bar{Q})$$

whereas the variance is given by

$$V_i = W_i^2 \sigma_{qq} + 2W_i \sum_j z_{ij}(\sigma_{qj} - p_j \sigma_{qq})$$
$$+ \sum_j \sum_k z_{ij} z_{ik}(\sigma_{jk} - p_k \sigma_{qj} - p_j \sigma_{qk} + p_j p_k \sigma_{qq}).$$

Again forming the Lagrangean

$$L_i = V_i - \lambda_i [E_i - W_i \bar{Q} - \sum_j z_{ij}(\mu_j - p_j \bar{Q})]$$

and setting the partial derivatives equal to zero, we obtain

$$\frac{\partial L_i}{\partial z_{ij}} = 2W_i(\sigma_{qj} - p_j \sigma_{qq}) + 2 \sum_k z_{ik}(\sigma_{jk} - p_k \sigma_{qj} - p_j \sigma_{qk} + p_j p_k \sigma_{qq})$$
$$- \lambda_i(\mu_j - p_j \bar{Q}) = 0$$

which can conveniently be written

$$\sum_k z_{ik}(\sigma_{jk} - p_k \sigma_{qj} - p_j \sigma_{qk} + p_j p_k \sigma_{qq}) = \frac{\lambda_i}{2}(\mu_j - p_j \bar{Q}) - (\sigma_{qj} - p_j \sigma_{qq})W_i$$
$$(j = 1, \ldots, n).$$

Summing each of these equations over i yields

$$\sum_k \sigma_{jk} - p_j \sum_k \sigma_{qk} = (\mu_j - p_j \bar{Q}) \sum_i \frac{\lambda_i}{2}.$$

On the LHS, the z_{ik} have disappeared because of the market clearing conditions $\sum_i z_{ij} = 1$, and a term $(\sigma_{qj} - p_j \sigma_{qq}) \sum_k p_k$ then drops out on both sides (recall that $\sum_i W_i = \sum_k p_k$). Solving the equation above for p_j then gives the valuation formula

$$p_j = \frac{\mu_j - Rb_j}{\bar{Q} - R \sum_k \sigma_{qk}}$$

where R and b_j are as before. Defining $\rho = \bar{Q} - R \sum_k \sigma_{qk}$, this can be written more simply as

(8) $$p_j = \frac{1}{\rho}(\mu_j - Rb_j)$$

in which form the similarity with the model of Chapter IV is obvious. The general structure of the formula is precisely as before, the only difference being that the discounting of the risk-adjusted mean is now made using an interest factor which is itself adjusted for risk. This latter adjustment is made in exactly the same way as the adjustment in expected company return, by subtracting the sum of the covariances weighted by the market risk aversion factor from the expected lending rate.

The summation of the covariance terms in the definition of ρ as $\bar{Q} - R \sum_k \sigma_{qk}$ does not include the variance σ_{qq} itself. Therefore, if the lending rate is uncorrelated with the X_j, the appropriate discounting rate is just equal to the expected lending rate. If company returns are predominantly positively correlated with the lending rate, the effect of the uncertainty of the lending rate is to raise share prices. This is of course in agreement with one's intuition. If the correlations are predominantly negative, however, lending is attractive as a complement to stockholdings and may therefore (because of the budget restraints) reduce the demand for shares, and thus lower their prices. But the most significant conclusion is that the market valuation *is* of the form (8), and only a slight modification is required when the assumption of a riskless lending rate is dropped. Thus, this assumption turns out to be far less crucial than one might initially suspect.

5.9.   We finally turn to an examination of the assumption of homogeneity of beliefs, i.e., the assumption that all investors agree in their estimates of the μ_j and σ_{jk}. Unfortunately, the conclusions we can draw from a model allowing heterogeneity of beliefs are less clear-cut than those derived above. Intuitively, one would expect the market valuation to reflect some sort of averaging of individual investors' probability estimates. This is indeed true, but the precise nature and effects of this averaging, i.e., the implied weighting factors, are somewhat difficult to characterize and interpret. This is because it is no longer possible to obtain the market value in explicit form, i.e., expressed in terms of given market parameters only.

Formally, we now let μ_{ij} and σ_{ijk} denote investor i's estimates of the means and covariance terms of company return. The mean and variance of his portfolio are therefore given by

$$E_i = rW_i + \sum_j z_{ij}(\mu_{ij} - rp_j),$$

$$V_i = \sum_j \sum_k z_{ij} z_{ik} \sigma_{ijk}.$$

By forming a Lagrangean as before and setting the partial derivatives equal to zero, we now obtain the demand functions as

$$\sum_k z_{ik} \sigma_{ijk} = \frac{\lambda_i}{2}(\mu_{ij} - rp_j)$$

for all i and j. Summing these equations over i gives

$$\sum_i \sum_k z_{ik}\sigma_{ijk} = \sum_i \frac{\lambda_i}{2}\mu_{ij} - rp_j \sum_i \frac{\lambda_i}{2},$$

which can be solved for p_j as

$$(9) \qquad p_j = \frac{1}{r}\left[\frac{1}{\sum_i \lambda_i}\sum_i \lambda_i\mu_{ij} - \frac{2}{\sum_i \lambda_i}\sum_i \sum_k z_{ik}\sigma_{ijk}\right].$$

If we now define the "surrogate" mean $\hat{\mu}_j$ and risk measure $\hat{b}_j$ as

$$\hat{\mu}_j = \frac{1}{\sum_i \lambda_i}\sum_i \lambda_i\mu_{ij}$$

$$\hat{b}_j = \sum_i \sum_k z_{ik}\sigma_{ijk}$$

(9) can clearly be written

$$p_j = \frac{1}{r}(\hat{\mu}_j - R\hat{b}_j)$$

where R as before equals $2/\sum \lambda_i$. Our first observation, and an important one, is that with heterogeneous beliefs it is still possible to express company value by the same kind of formula as that developed in Chapter IV, but in terms of the surrogate mean and risk measure as defined above.

Taking a closer look at these surrogate measures, we first observe that by changing the order of summation, $\hat{b}_j$ can alternatively be written

$$\hat{b}_j = \sum_k \sum_i z_{ik}\sigma_{ijk}.$$

From this we see that the surrogate risk measure is obtained as the sum of the weighted averages of each investor's estimate of the covariance terms. More formally, these weighted averages are defined by

$$\hat{\sigma}_{jk} = \sum_i z_{ik}\sigma_{ijk}$$

and it then follows that

$$\hat{b}_j = \sum_k \hat{\sigma}_{jk}.$$

The weighting factors for the covariance estimates are simply the fractions owned of each firm. This means that the wealthier the investor, or the lower the position of his risk aversion function, the more weight carried by his estimates of the covariance terms.

Turning to the surrogate for the expected return, $\hat{\mu}_j$, we observe that this also represents a weighted average of individual estimates of expected return. The weights are equal to λ_i. We have seen before that $1/\lambda_i$ gives a measure of the strength of the investor's risk aversion; λ_i can therefore be interpreted as a measure of his risk *tolerance*. Recognizing this more explicitly, define $T_i = \lambda_i$ and $T = \sum T_i$; then $\hat{\mu}_j$ can be expressed as

$$\hat{\mu}_j = \frac{1}{T} \sum_i T_i \mu_{ij}.$$

Assuming risk aversion to be decreasing with wealth, we again conclude that the larger the investor's wealth, or the lower the position of his risk aversion function, the more weight does his estimate of expected return carry.

5.10. One important question suggested by these considerations is whether we would expect any systematic bias in investors' estimates. Specifically, would we expect wealthy investors, or investors with low risk aversion, to have estimates which are consistently different from those of other investors? Suppose that we asked a number of very wealthy investors about their estimates μ_{ij} and σ_{ijk} and contrasted this with a random sample. Would we expect the answers to be significantly different?

In considering any individual investor's portfolio selection, we assumed that he could separate in his mind the specification of his opportunities from the specification of his preferences. But this need not necessarily mean that no *statistical* dependence exists across investors. There is, for example, the possibility that persons who would make very conservative decisions (given their estimates μ_{ij} and σ_{ijk}) would also tend to have high estimates of the variance-covariance terms, or low estimates of the means in the first place. If such systematic effects are absent, the effect of heterogeneity would be much less pronounced. Furthermore, in order to predict the value of a firm we would then need only an "everyman's" estimate, in the sense that the average estimates from a randomly selected sample would give unbiased estimates of the surrogate measures $\hat{\mu}_j$ and $\hat{b}_j$.

Whether there are, in fact, such statistical relationships between conservatism of estimates and risk aversion and wealth level is an empirical problem about which we know little or nothing. At present, we can only hope that they will be largely absent, but there does not seem to be any point in pursuing further speculations.

The question we are concerned with is: What are the effects of allowing heterogeneous beliefs? Formulated this way, the question is not specific enough to allow very specific answers. It is too easy (and not very useful) to say that because homogeneity of beliefs is an unrealistic assumption, results derived from a model based on it must be wrong or useless. This is only to beg such questions as: Wrong in what ways? Wrong or useless relative to what? How wrong? Wrong or useless for what purposes? For example, one of the main purposes of our theory is to explore its implications for the firm's optimal investment criteria. As we shall see in Chapter VII, these criteria depend only on the *changes* in the means and covariance terms caused by an investment, not on their absolute value. Consequently, if investors are largely agreed in their assessments of these changes—which does not seem so unrealistic—it does not matter whether they otherwise agree or disagree. This example is meant to illustrate that meaningful answers can only be given to clearly formulated objections.

5.11. In discussing the importance of heterogeneity of beliefs, there are two kinds of considerations to take into account. What we have been concerned with so far are the effects of a given amount of heterogeneity. The other major consideration is the degree to which beliefs are in fact heterogeneous. The question is whether homogeneity of beliefs, at least as an approximation, is such a terribly unrealistic assumption after all. Some brief comments may be in order.

To begin with, it may be argued that we are merely assuming that all investors have available to them the same information about companies and the economy. It seems difficult to escape the logical conclusion that two investors with the same information cannot arrive at different estimates of the probabilities involved. The validity of this statement depends, of course, on just how broadly we define "information." In any event, it is clear that differences in probability estimates must arise primarily because of differences in information. So we might ask how unrealistic an hypothesis of equal information might be.

It should be kept in mind that the portfolio decisions and resulting valuation model with which we are concerned in this book are of a relatively long-term nature. We are not particularly interested in day-to-day speculative decisions based on short-run market fluctuations, nor are we concerned with these fluctuations themselves. As a consequence, we are interested in basic information about the companies' economic activity, and not the various hot tips and rumors that circulate on Wall Street, which by their nature are available to a chosen few.

Concentrating on this more basic information, we can probably say that all investors have *access* to the same information if they want it. However, investors clearly differ considerably with respect to the amount of information collecting and processing they are prepared to go through. It is neither feasible nor rational for the small personal investor to engage in detailed security analysis, while such institutional investors as trusts, mutual funds, and insurance companies spend considerable efforts on security analysis. Nobody would be surprised if estimates by such different groups turned out to differ considerably, although it is again difficult to say whether any systematic biases would be involved. However, within the group of professional security analysts and institutional investors, we would reasonably expect estimates to be fairly homogeneous. It is interesting to speculate that as more and more stock transactions are controlled by such institutional investors, our model's assumption of homogeneity of beliefs may come closer to holding. In other words, we may argue that the quantitative role of those with different opinions has been reduced to the extent that their effect on security prices is insignificant.

6 Efficiency

of Security Markets

6.1. In the preceding chapters we have developed a model of the pricing and allocation of securities in a competitive market. As far as the pricing is concerned, we shall obviously be interested in pursuing further the model's implications for corporate decision making. Before doing so, however, we shall consider some welfare theoretical aspects of the model. In a sense, this discussion represents a digression from the main line of argument of the book, but there are good reasons for including it. First, the results to be presented are important in themselves, as they differ considerably from the main results of classical welfare theory under certainty. Second, the results may provide some insight into certain observed phenomena in existing security market arrangements.

6.2. It is useful to start our analysis with a brief review of the classical theory of the efficiency of a commodity exchange market under certainty. This will help to clarify basic concepts and establish a certain analytical apparatus.

Consider an economy of m persons and n commodities, and let x_{ij} be the amount of commodity j received by person i. The total supply of each commodity is fixed, so that any allocation must satisfy the market clearing conditions

(1)
$$\sum_i x_{ij} = v_j \qquad (j = 1, \ldots, n)$$

where v_j is the given supply of commodity j. Any allocation satisfying (1) is called a feasible allocation.

Each person is assumed to have a preference ordering over commodity combinations allocated to him which can be represented by a concave utility function

$$U_i = f_i(x_{i1}, \ldots, x_{in}).$$

Now consider two allocations x_{ij}^1 and x_{ij}^2 with corresponding utility levels U_i^1 and U_i^2. We say that the allocation x_{ij}^1 *dominates* the allocation x_{ij}^2 if $U_i^1 \geq U_i^2$ for all i and $U_i^1 > U_i^2$ for at least one i. Thus, an allocation dominates another if it gives one or more persons a higher utility level without giving any person a lower utility level. A reasonable condition to impose on an allocation is that it should not be dominated by another allocation; otherwise the allocation would represent an inefficient use of the given resources. This leads us to require that an allocation be *efficient*, or *Pareto-optimal*, in the sense that there should exist no other feasible allocation which dominates it.

The concept of Pareto-optimality is illustrated in Figure 7 for a case involving two persons. When the utility functions are concave (i.e., represented by indifference curves which are convex to the origin), the set of feasible allocations generate a set of utility levels (U_1, U_2) which is convex (the shaded area). Any point inside this set, such as P, is inefficient, since it is

FIGURE 7

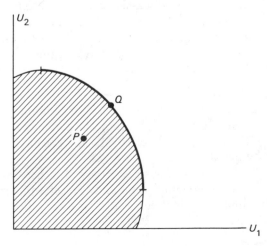

possible to find another allocation which is preferred by both persons. Along the northeast boundary of the set, however, no such reallocation is possible— any movement from a point such as Q must lead to a less preferred position for at least one of the persons.

Algebraically, we can formulate the condition of Pareto-optimality as follows. Let the allocation x_{ij} be changed to $x_{ij} + dx_{ij}$. Then the change in person i's utility is

$$dU_i = \sum_j f_{ij} dx_{ij} \qquad\qquad (i = 1, \ldots, m)$$

where f_{ij} denotes the partial derivative $\partial f_i / \partial x_{ij}$. Any such reallocation must clearly satisfy the market clearing conditions, i.e., we must have

(2) $$\sum_i dx_{ij} = 0 \qquad\qquad (j = 1, \ldots, n).$$

The allocation x_{ij} is then Pareto-optimal if and only if the dU_i are not all positive (or if they are all zero).

The following theorem is useful in determining the set of Pareto-optimal allocations.

THEOREM.   *An allocation is Pareto-optimal if and only if*

(3) $$k_i f_{ij} - f_{1j} \qquad\qquad (i = 1, \ldots, m;\ j = 1, \ldots, n)$$

where $k_1 = 1$ and $k_2, \ldots, k_m$ are arbitrary positive constants.

The theorem is a special case of the Kuhn-Tucker theorem, and can also be proved directly in a simple manner. We shall indicate the ideas behind the proof, following Borch [2].

Let us change the allocation from x_{ij} to $x_{ij} + dx_{ij}$. If the conditions (3) are fulfilled, we have

$$k_i dU_i = \sum_j f_{1j} dx_{ij}$$

and hence, in view of (2),

$$\sum_i k_i dU_i = \sum_i \sum_j f_{1j} dx_{ij} = \sum_j f_{1j} \sum_i dx_{ij} = 0.$$

But with the $k_i > 0$, this implies that the dU_i cannot all be of the same sign (unless they are all zero).

To demonstrate the necessity of the conditions, let $dx_{ij} = 0$ for $i > 2, j > 2$. We must then have

$$dx_{21} = -dx_{11}, \qquad dx_{22} = -dx_{12}.$$

The changes in utility are

$$dU_1 = f_{11}dx_{11} + f_{12}dx_{12}$$
$$dU_2 = -(f_{21}dx_{11} + f_{22}dx_{12}).$$

When the allocation is Pareto-optimal, the product of the utility changes must be nonpositive, hence

$$(f_{11}dx_{11} + f_{12}dx_{12})(f_{21}dx_{11} + f_{22}dx_{12}) \geq 0$$

or

$$f_{11}f_{21}(dx_{11})^2 + (f_{12}f_{21} + f_{11}f_{22})dx_{11}dx_{12}$$
$$+ f_{12}f_{22}(dx_{12})^2 \geq 0.$$

From the theory of quadratic forms we know that a necessary condition for this inequality to be satisfied is that

$$f_{11}f_{21}f_{12}f_{22} - \tfrac{1}{4}(f_{12}f_{21} + f_{11}f_{22})^2 \geq 0$$

which can be written

$$(f_{12}f_{21} - f_{11}f_{22})^2 \leq 0.$$

This can only hold if

$$\frac{f_{11}}{f_{21}} = \frac{f_{12}}{f_{22}}$$

i.e., when conditions (3) are fulfilled. Hence, it follows that (3) is also a necessary condition for Pareto-optimality.

If the utility functions are concave (i.e., have convex indifference curves), the conditions (3) also represent conditions for a maximum of $\sum_i k_i U_i$ subject to the market clearing conditions. For by forming the Lagrangean

$$L = \sum_i k_i U_i + \sum_j \lambda_j(v_j - \sum_i x_{ij})$$

we get the first-order conditions for a maximum

$$\frac{\partial L}{\partial x_{ij}} = k_i f_{ij} - \lambda_j = 0 \qquad (i = 1, \ldots, m; j = 1, \ldots, n)$$

which are identical with (3). Thus, the theorem might just as well have said that an allocation is Pareto-optimal if and only if it maximizes a positively weighted sum of individual utilities. The theorem can then easily be interpreted geometrically: Any point along the northeast boundary of the feasible set in Figure 7 represents the maximum of a positively weighted sum $U_1 + kU_2$; by letting k vary we obtain the set of all Pareto-optimal allocations.

6.3.   One of the central results of classical equilibrium theory is that if our persons organize the commodity allocation by means of trading at prices p_j which clear all markets, then the resulting allocation is Pareto-optimal. Conversely, any Pareto-optimal allocation can be obtained by specifying an initial allocation y_{ij} and a set of prices p_j and letting people trade at these prices.

In a competitive market, the demand of person i is determined by his attempt to maximize $U_i = f_i(x_{i1}, \ldots, x_{in})$ subject to his budget condition

$$\sum_j p_j x_{ij} = \sum_j p_j y_{ij}.$$

The solution to this problem is given by the well known conditions

$$f_{ij} = \lambda_i p_j \qquad (i = 1, \ldots, m; \ j = 1, \ldots, n)$$

where λ_i is a Lagrangean multiplier. These conditions can be written

$$\frac{\lambda_1}{\lambda_i} f_{ij} = f_{1j}$$

and are then seen to be identical with conditions (3). Hence the market allocation is Pareto-optimal. This result provides the basic theoretical justification for a competitive market economy. As we shall see, life is not so simple when uncertainty is introduced.

6.4.   Let us return to an examination of our model of security market equilibrium. We recall that person i's final wealth was defined by the variable

(4) $$Y_i = rm_i + \sum_j z_{ij}(X_j - rd_j)$$

and that the equations describing his demand were

(5) $$\mathcal{E}[u_i'(Y_i)(X_j - rp_j - rd_j)] = 0 \qquad (j = 1, \ldots, n)$$

and the budget equation

$$W_i = m_i + \sum_j z_{ij} p_j.$$

Now consider a reallocation dz_{ij} and dm_i. From the market clearing conditions such a reallocation must satisfy

(6)
$$\sum_i dz_{ij} = 0 \qquad (j = 1, \ldots, n)$$
$$\sum_i dm_i = 0.$$

Expected utility is

$$U_i = \mathcal{E}[u_i(Y_i)],$$

so that the change in utility is

$$dU_i = \mathcal{E}[u_i'(Y_i)dY_i]$$
$$= \mathcal{E}[u_i'(Y_i)(rdm_i + \sum_j (X_j - rd_j)dz_{ij})]$$
$$= r\mathcal{E}[u_i'(Y_i)]dm_i + \sum_j \mathcal{E}[u_i'(Y_i)(X_j - rd_j)]dz_{ij}.$$

From (5) we have

$$\mathcal{E}[u_i'(Y_i)(X_j - rd_j)] = rp_j\mathcal{E}[u_i'(Y_i)],$$

hence

$$dU_i = r\mathcal{E}[u_i'(Y_i)](dm_i + \sum_j p_j dz_{ij})$$

or

$$\alpha_i dU_i = dm_i + \sum_j p_j dz_{ij}$$

where $\alpha_i = 1/r\mathcal{E}[u_i'(Y_i)]$. Summing over i, we obtain, in view of (6),

$$\sum_i \alpha_i dU_i = \sum_i dm_i + \sum_i \sum_j p_j dz_{ij} = 0.$$

Since the $\alpha_i > 0$, we conclude that the dU_i are not all of the same sign, so that the market determines a Pareto-optimal allocation of stocks and bonds.

6.5.   From the analysis above we seem to be entitled to conclude that our market does its job efficiently. A little reflection shows that this statement requires major qualifications, however, the nature of which must be clearly understood.

The most general way of describing a scheme for allocating returns is to specify a set of functions, one for each investor,

$$Y_i = g_i(X_1, \ldots, X_n),$$

which tells us how much investor i is to receive when payments from the companies are $X_1, \ldots, X_n$. Such a function is called a *sharing rule*. There do not seem to be any a priori reasons for imposing restrictions on the form of these sharing rules. However, when the market is restricted to trading only in bonds and ordinary shares, then a restriction *is* imposed on the sharing rules. The restriction arises because ordinary shares give the owner a proportional interest in a company, whereas some nonproportional arrangement might actually be preferable. From the expression (4) we see that our market allows *linear* sharing rules only, whereas in a completely general arrangement the sharing rules may have any form. It is obvious that such a restriction must in general lead to a suboptimal allocation of risk.

By using the concept of state of the world, in which a set of values for the $X_j = X_j(\theta)$ is specified for each of the states of the world θ, the sharing rules can be written simply as a set of functions $Y_i(\theta)$, the values of which give the amount received by person i in state θ. In these terms, person i's expected utility is given by $U_i = \sum_\theta u_i(Y_i(\theta)) f(\theta)$, where $f(\theta)$ is the probability distribution over states of the world. If we define $W(\theta) = \sum_j X_j(\theta)$ as total or aggregate yield in state θ, then the sharing rules must satisfy

(7) $$\sum_i Y_i(\theta) = W(\theta)$$

for every θ.

As in the commodity exchange model, we shall require, as a minimal efficiency condition, that the sharing rules give a Pareto-optimal risk allocation. This means that we want to specify the sharing rules which maximize a positively weighted sum $\sum_i k_i U_i$ subject to (7). The conditions for such a maximum can be derived by forming the Lagrangean

$$L = \sum_i k_i U_i + \sum_\theta \lambda(\theta)[W(\theta) - \sum_i Y_i(\theta)]$$

and setting the partial derivatives equal to zero:

$$\frac{\partial L}{\partial Y_i(\theta)} = k_i u_i'(Y_i(\theta)) f(\theta) - \lambda(\theta) = 0$$

for every i and θ. We can rewrite these conditions in more convenient form as

(8) $$k_i u_i'(Y_i(\theta)) = u_1'(Y_1(\theta)).$$

We shall examine some of the implications of these conditions.

6.6. Consider first a situation in which person 1 is risk neutral, while all others are risk averse. This means that $u_1'(Y_1(\theta))$ is a constant function, or, in other words, that the RHS of (8) is the same for every θ. The functions u_i', however, are not constant functions for $i \neq 1$; therefore (8) cannot be satisfied unless the Y_i themselves are the same for every θ, say $Y_i = a_i$. It then follows from (7) that Y_1 is given by $Y_1 = W - \sum_{i \neq 1} a_i$. What this means is simply that the risk neutral investor should carry all the risk, while none should be borne by the others.

In the following we shall disregard the case of risk neutral investors, however, and study some applications of the conditions (8) when the utility functions exhibit risk aversion.

6.7. A particularly simple case occurs when all utility functions are the simple logarithmic $u_i(Y_i) = \ln Y_i$. Here $u_i' = 1/Y_i$, so that (8) requires

$$\frac{k_i}{Y_i} = \frac{1}{Y_1},$$

or

$$Y_i = k_i Y_1.$$

Summing over i and using (7) we then have

$$\sum_i Y_i = Y_1 \sum_i k_i = W,$$

from which we obtain the sharing rules as

$$Y_i = \frac{k_i}{\sum_i k_i} W.$$

Thus, Pareto-optimality requires a constant fraction of total return to each investor. Such an allocation can evidently be effected by a stock market; there will not even be room for a riskless asset. If firms issue bonds (which must be owned by somebody), Pareto-optimality cannot be achieved; investors will prefer to have company returns paid as dividends rather than interest.

6.8. In this example, the amount received by an individual depends only on aggregate return and not on its composition. This result must actually hold for *any* set of utility functions. To show this, differentiate (7) and (8) with respect to X_j:

(9)
$$\sum_i \frac{\partial Y_i}{\partial X_j} = 1$$

(10)
$$k_i u_i''(Y_i) \frac{\partial Y_i}{\partial X_j} = u_1''(Y_1) \frac{\partial Y_1}{\partial X_j}.$$

From (10) we get

$$\frac{\partial Y_i}{\partial X_j} = u_1''(Y_1) \frac{\partial Y_1}{\partial X_j} \frac{1}{k_i u_i''(Y_i)}.$$

By summing over i, we obtain, in view of (9),

$$\sum_i \frac{\partial Y_i}{\partial X_j} = u_1''(Y_1) \frac{\partial Y_1}{\partial X_j} \sum_i \frac{1}{k_i u_i''(Y_i)} = 1.$$

We then have in general

$$\frac{\partial Y_i}{\partial X_j} = \frac{\dfrac{1}{k_i u_i''(Y_i)}}{\displaystyle\sum_i \frac{1}{k_i u_i''(Y_i)}}.$$

The RHS does not depend on j. This means that Y_i depends on the scalar variable $W = \sum_j X_j$ only.

The fact that Y_i is a function of W alone means that any Pareto-optimal allocation can be effected by pooling all companies into one big mutual fund and then specifying some rule as to how the return of the mutual fund should be divided among investors. In our competitive model we found that since the z_{ij} were the same for all j, the market allocation was actually equivalent to such an arrangement. This in itself is clearly not sufficient for Pareto-optimality, however.

The intuitive reason why any Pareto-optimal sharing rule requires that payments to individuals depend only on aggregate return and not on its composition can be seen by considering a simple example. Suppose there were two firms with return patterns over two states of the world as follows:

	State	
Company	1	2
1	5	10
2	10	5
W	15	15

but the sharing rules were such that the allocation to individuals was

	State	
Person	1	2
1	7	8
2	8	7
W	15	15

rather than giving each the same in both states. The situation is here that from the point of view of the economy as a whole there is no uncertainty: total return is 15 no matter what state obtains. However, the sharing rules have created an "artificial" uncertainty for both investors. Sharing rules which avoid this must clearly be superior.

6.9.   As a second illustration, consider the case where all investors have quadratic utility functions $u_i(Y_i) = Y_i - c_i Y_i^2$. Conditions (8) then become

$$k_i(1 - 2c_i Y_i) = 1 - 2c_1 Y_1,$$

from which we get

$$Y_i = \frac{1}{2c_i} - \frac{1}{2c_i k_i}(1 - 2c_1 Y_1)$$

and hence

$$\sum_i Y_i = \sum_i \frac{1}{2c_i} - (1 - 2c_1 Y_1) \sum_i \frac{1}{2c_i k_i} = W.$$

Substituting back into the first equation, we can then solve for Y_i as

(11)
$$Y_i = \frac{1}{2c_i} - \frac{\frac{1}{c_i k_i}}{\sum_i \frac{1}{c_i k_i}} \left(\sum_i \frac{1}{2c_i} - W \right).$$

The noteworthy property of this relationship is that Y_i is a linear function of W, i.e., it can be written in the form

$$Y_i = a_i + b_i W.$$

This means that in this case a Pareto-optimal arrangement can also be effected by means of a market for stocks and bonds. Because of the non-random elements a_i, the existence of a riskless asset is essential, and the stock allocation must clearly be such that every investor owns the same fraction of the stock of each company.

It is instructive to look at the application of the sharing rules (11) to the numerical example used in Chapter IV. In the example, the coefficients of the utility functions were $c_1 = 1/5$, $c_2 = 1/6$. Using these values and writing $k_2 = k$, the sharing rule for person 1 becomes

$$Y_1 = \frac{15 - 5k(3 - W)}{6 + 5k}.$$

Thus, the amount received by person 1 in each of the three states of the world are

(12)
$$Y_1(1) = \frac{15 - 10k}{6 + 5k}$$

$$Y_1(2) = \frac{15 - 5k}{6 + 5k}$$

$$Y_1(3) = \frac{15}{6 + 5k}$$

while person 2 receives the remainder.

If an allocation does not satisfy the conditions above for some k, it is not Pareto-optimal; conversely, any allocation which does satisfy them for some k is Pareto-optimal. We now observe that by setting $k = 378/275$ we obtain precisely the same solution as we found in Chapter IV for the competitive market allocation. This clearly means that the market solution was, after all, Pareto-optimal. Our last example, and results to be derived later, will show that this is due to the particular utility functions assumed in the example.

6.10. Consider finally the risk sharing by two persons with utility functions

$$u_1(Y_1) = 2Y_1^{1/2}, \qquad u_2(Y_2) = \tfrac{4}{3}Y_2^{3/4}.$$

Condition (8) becomes in this case

$$Y_1^{-1/2} = kY_2^{-1/4}.$$

Substituting $Y_2 = W - Y_1$ and solving for Y_1, we obtain the sharing rule

(13) $$Y_1 = (2hW + h^2)^{1/2} - h,$$

where $h = k^{-4}/2 > 0$. Since the sharing rule is not linear, it cannot be effected by means of stocks and bonds. From the form of the sharing rule it is fairly obvious that no other familiar securities can effect it either.

6.11. The statement in the preceding paragraph requires one qualification that has to do with the number of distinct states of the world as compared with the number of distinct securities. The meaning of this is best clarified by an example.

Suppose there are two companies with return patterns over three states of the world as follows:

	State		
Company	1	2	3
1	0	2	4
2	2	4	8
W	2	6	12

If the sharing rule for person 1 is given by (13) and h is set equal to 1/2, the allocation should be

	State		
Person	1	2	3
1	1	2	3
2	1	4	9
W	2	6	12

It is easy to see that this allocation can be effected by using bonds and ordinary shares only. The way this must be done is to set $z_{11} = 1/2$, $z_{12} = 0$, $m_1 = 1$; $z_{21} = 1/2$, $z_{22} = 1$, $m_2 = 1$; in other words, person 2 has a 50 per cent interest in company 1, owns company 2 outright, and issues a note to person 1 for one unit of money, while person 1, in addition to the IOU from person 2, owns the remaining 50 per cent of company 1.

The reason why such an arrangement works out in this case is that there are as many securities (bonds and two kinds of stock) as there are states of the world. The stock and bond allocation given above is clearly the solution (for person 1) of the equations

$$m_1 + \quad\quad 2z_{12} = 1$$
$$m_1 + 2z_{11} + 4z_{12} = 2$$
$$m_1 + 4z_{11} + 8z_{12} = 3.$$

In general, to determine a stock-bond allocation resulting in any given yield pattern, we would have a set of as many linear equations as there are states of the world in as many variables as there are securities. Except for cases of linear dependence, such a system can have a solution only if the number of securities is at least as large as the number of states of the world. Whether this condition can be said to be satisfied in some sense in reality is a question to which we shall have to return.

However, even if some given Pareto-optimal allocation can be brought about by *some* allocation of stocks and bonds, it may not be possible to get it as the outcome of *market* transactions. If a market mechanism allocates to person 1 the amounts y_1, y_2, y_3 in three states of the world, it is Pareto-optimal *only* if there exists an h such that

$$(4h + h^2)^{1/2} - h = y_1$$
$$(12h + h^2)^{1/2} - h = y_2$$
$$(24h + h^2)^{1/2} - h = y_3.$$

This is three equations in just one variable h, and will in general have no solution. If the market allocation results in $y_1 = 1$, then the only way it can be Pareto-optimal is by at the same time giving $y_2 = 2$ and $y_3 = 3$. But there will no doubt exist markets where the initial allocation and the probability distribution for θ is such that the trading gives an allocation different from that (in the example we would have five degrees of freedom—two probabilities and three figures from the initial allocation—to determine two y's such that the system above becomes inconsistent). This means that the market allocation will, except in rare cases of coincidence, be suboptimal.

In the example, the expected utilities corresponding to the allocation given are $U_1 = 2.57$ and $U_2 = 3.35$. Person 1 would obtain precisely the same utility with an allocation such as $Y_1(1) = 1$, $Y_1(2) = 1.5$, $Y_1(3) = 3.695$. There is no reason why there should not be markets resulting in this kind of pattern. However, this allocation gives person 2 a utility of only 3.33, and is therefore inferior to the one given.

6.12. In our examples we found two cases where the Pareto-optimal sharing rules were linear (and hence could be effected by means of bonds and ordinary shares), and one case where this (in general) was impossible. It is obviously of considerable interest to determine more fully the conditions under which the optimal sharing rules are linear. We shall demonstrate how this can be done.

The optimality conditions are as before

$$(14) \qquad\qquad k_i u_i'(Y_i) = u_1'(Y_1) \qquad\qquad (i = 2, \ldots, n)$$

and the linearity conditions can be written

$$(15) \qquad\qquad Y_i = a_i + b_i W,$$

where the a_i and b_i may depend on the k_i. These conditions are to be considered as defining restrictions on the form of the functions $u_i'(Y_i)$.

We have already seen that if one individual, say person 1, is risk neutral, then

$$Y_1 = W - \sum_{i \neq 1} a_i$$

$$Y_i = a_i \qquad\qquad (i = 2, \ldots, n).$$

Such an arrangement can clearly be effected by stocks and bonds by giving person 1 all the risky stocks and having him issue riskless bonds to everybody else. Apart from the case of risk neutral individuals, however, we shall show that a necessary and sufficient condition for (14) and (15) to be satisfied is that *all* utility functions are such that

$$(16) \qquad\qquad -\frac{u_i'(Y_i)}{u_i''(Y_i)} = \alpha_i + \beta Y_i.$$

The function $-u'(Y)/u''(Y)$ is the inverse of the risk aversion function, and is sometimes referred to as the risk tolerance function. Thus, we require risk tolerance to be linear and have the *same* slope for all individuals. Apart from linear transformations, the following (and only the following) forms of utility functions satisfy this condition (for $\alpha_i \neq 0$):

Exponential: $u_i(Y_i) = -e^{-Y_i/\alpha_i}$ (for $\beta = 0$)

Logarithmic: $u_i(Y_i) = \ln (Y_i + \alpha_i)$ (for $\beta = 1$)

Power: $u_i(Y_i) = \dfrac{1}{\beta - 1}(\alpha_i + \beta Y_i)^{1 - 1/\beta}$ (otherwise).

Quadratic utility functions are included in this set as the special case $\beta = -1$. When $\alpha_i = 0$, the set reduces to $u_i(Y_i) = \ln Y_i$ and $u_i(Y_i) = Y_i^{1-1/\beta}$.

It must be emphasized that the conditions (16) are very strong—each and every utility function must belong to a rather restricted class of functions. If one individual has an exponential utility function, so must everybody else; the same is true of the logarithmic. If one utility function is a power function, then all others must also be power functions with the *same* power. Mixing of functions with different power (as in the example given earlier) or mixing of, say, logarithmic and power functions, will not give linear sharing rules.

To demonstrate the necessity of (16), differentiate (14) with respect to W and k_i, respectively:

$$k_i u_i''(Y_i)b_i = u_1''(Y_1)b_1$$
$$u_i'(Y_i) + k_i u_i''(Y_i)(a_{ii} + b_{ii}W) = u_1''(Y_1)(a_{1i} + b_{1i}W),$$

where a_{rs} denotes the derivative of a_r with respect to k_s. Substituting from the first equation into the second, using the relation $W = (Y_i - a_i)/b_i$ obtained from (14), and rearranging, we obtain

(17) $$-\frac{u_i'(Y_i)}{u_i''(Y_i)} = \alpha_i + \beta_i Y_i,$$

where α_i and β_i are functions of the k_i.

Solving the differential equation (17) for u_i', we get, except for a constant of integration,

$$u_i'(Y_i) = e^{-Y_i/\alpha_i} \qquad \text{(for } \beta_i = 0)$$
$$u_i'(Y_i) = (\alpha_i + \beta_i Y_i)^{-1/\beta_i} \qquad \text{(otherwise).}$$

In the first case, it is trivial to verify that the Pareto-optimal sharing rules are linear. In the second case, the optimality conditions become

$$k_i(\alpha_i + \beta_i Y_i)^{-1/\beta_i} = (\alpha_1 + \beta_1 Y_1)^{-1/\beta_1}$$

and these give linear sharing rules if and only if the β_i are all equal. This also establishes the sufficiency of condition (16).

6.13. Our results so far have been essentially negative. Only under exceedingly restrictive assumptions about investors' preferences can a competitive market for stocks and bonds (or other familiar securities) lead to a Pareto-optimal risk allocation. It is then natural to ask whether the central result of classical equilibrium theory can be saved by introducing securities different from those we are used to. From our discussion of the relationship between the number of different securities and the number of different states of the world, it is clear that an arbitrary return pattern can be effected by means of securities only if their number is at least as large as the number of states of the world. What this suggests is that the natural instruments of allocation are not really claims to the return of different companies, but rather claims to return in different states of the world. A natural set of securities to consider is then a set of certificates, one for each state of the world, which will pay one unit of money if that particular state occurs, and nothing otherwise. Such securities were originally suggested by Arrow [1], and are therefore often referred to as Arrow certificates. Another term for them is state contingent claims. We shall show that a competitive market for such securities will indeed result in a Pareto-optimal risk allocation.

Denote by $p(\theta)$ the price of a certificate paying one dollar if and only if state θ occurs, and let $x_i(\theta)$ be the number of such certificates purchased by individual i. This means that his income in state θ is precisely equal to $x_i(\theta)$, i.e.,

$$Y_i(\theta) = x_i(\theta).$$

His budget restraint can then be written

(18) $$\sum_\theta p(\theta)x_i(\theta) = W_i,$$

so that his problem is to maximize $\mathcal{E}[u_i(Y_i)] = \sum_\theta u_i(x_i(\theta))f(\theta)$ subject to (18). Forming the Lagrangean

$$L_i = \sum_\theta u_i(x_i(\theta))f(\theta) + \lambda_i[W_i - \sum_\theta p(\theta)x_i(\theta)]$$

and setting the derivatives with respect to the $x_i(\theta)$ equal to zero, we obtain the demand relations

(19) $$\frac{\partial L_i}{\partial x_i(\theta)} = u_i'(x_i(\theta))f(\theta) - \lambda_i p(\theta) = 0$$

for all θ and i. From these conditions it follows that

$$\frac{\lambda_1}{\lambda_i} u_i'(Y_i(\theta)) = u_1'(Y_1(\theta))$$

which is identical with conditions (8) and hence implies Pareto-optimality.

6.14. It is instructive to compare the equilibrium allocation in a market for Arrow certificates with that in a market for stocks and bonds.

Consider again the numerical example of Chapter IV. The return patterns for the two companies were given by

		State	
Company	*1*	*2*	*3*
1	0	1	1
2	1	1	2
W	1	2	3
Probability	1/2	1/4	1/4

This table also gives the supply of Arrow certificates; thus, for example, there will be a total of three state-3-certificates, one being issued by company 1 (or its owners) and two by company 2.

Consider now person 1, whose marginal utility function was $u'_1 = 1 - (2/5)Y_1$. The first-order conditions (19) are then

$$\tfrac{1}{2}(1 - \tfrac{2}{5}x_1(1)) = \lambda_1 p(1)$$
$$\tfrac{1}{4}(1 - \tfrac{2}{5}x_1(2)) = \lambda_1 p(2)$$
$$\tfrac{1}{4}(1 - \tfrac{2}{5}x_1(3)) = \lambda_1 p(3)$$

from which we obtain, through elimination of λ_1,

$$\frac{p(2)}{p(1)} = \frac{1 - \tfrac{2}{5}x_1(2)}{2 - \tfrac{4}{5}x_1(1)}$$
$$\frac{p(3)}{p(1)} = \frac{1 - \tfrac{2}{5}x_1(3)}{2 - \tfrac{4}{5}x_1(1)}.$$

We know that the market allocation will be Pareto-optimal, and can therefore make use of the optimality conditions (12) to determine

$$\frac{p(2)}{p(1)} = \frac{1 - \dfrac{2}{5}\dfrac{15 - 5k}{6 + 5k}}{2 - \dfrac{4}{5}\dfrac{15 - 10k}{6 + 5k}} = \frac{7}{18}$$

$$\frac{p(3)}{p(1)} = \frac{1 - \dfrac{2}{5}\dfrac{15}{6 + 5k}}{2 - \dfrac{4}{5}\dfrac{15 - 10k}{6 + 5k}} = \frac{5}{18}.$$

Since only relative prices are determined, the prices can be normalized in a suitable manner. We observe that if we buy one of each Arrow certificate we will receive one dollar with certainty. Such a package will cost $\sum_\theta p(\theta)$ and is clearly equivalent to a riskless asset. For purposes of comparison with the stock-bond model, it is then natural to normalize the prices so that

$$\sum_\theta p(\theta) = \frac{1}{r}.$$

In our example, $r = 1$, so that the normalized prices become

$$p(1) = \tfrac{18}{30}, \quad p(2) = \tfrac{7}{30}, \quad p(3) = \tfrac{5}{30}.$$

These prices reflect partly the differences in probability of occurrence of the different states, and partly the decreasing marginal utility of increasing total return.

Assuming as before that the initial allocation is such that person 1 owns company 1 and person 2 owns company 2, initial wealths are

$$W_1 = p(2) + p(3) = \tfrac{2}{5}$$
$$W_2 = p(1) + p(2) + 2p(3) = \tfrac{7}{6}$$

just as in the stock-bond model. It is also easy to verify that the solution for the $x_i(\theta)$ gives precisely the same allocation of returns. Of course, we knew that with quadratic utility functions the stock-bond market allocation would be Pareto-optimal; the example seems to indicate that the allocations under the two regimes will actually be identical.

6.15.   Of course, in the real world, Arrow certificates in pure form do not exist. This in itself is not so important as the requirement that the number of securities be as large as the number of states of the world. The question then arises: How many states of the world are there? In principle, this is easy to answer. Since the Pareto-optimal allocations depend on aggregate return only—not its distribution among firms—there are as many relevant states of the world as there are distinct possibilities for the value of aggregate return. In practice, it would probably be most natural to describe aggregate return in terms of a continuous probability distribution, in which case the number of different states is infinitely large. Trading in a limited number of securities will then lead to a suboptimal risk allocation. If new securities were introduced we would expect the market to approach, but never reach, a full optimum.

This possibility has an interesting implication. Real world security markets never seem to be in a state of stable equilibrium; prices fluctuate all the time. One explanation of this is that the market never has time to settle down to an equilibrium position before external conditions change and initiate a new set of disturbances. Borch [3] has suggested another explanation based on the considerations above: the suboptimality of a market with a finite number of securities gives room for incentive for brokers and other promoters to create a steady flow of new securities, and thus keep the market moving all the time. Brokers of various sorts appear to be most common in markets where uncertainty is prevalent. This might be taken as evidence that a competitive market mechanism does not function properly in such markets; if it did, brokers would be unnecessary middlemen.

In a sense, our concept of optimality is somewhat limited, in that it does not take into account the transaction costs associated with a large number of securities. If it did, we would no doubt find that some finite number of securities would strike the proper balance between transaction costs and ability to adapt yield patterns to individual preferences. Whether actual security markets are able to effect this balance is of course another question.

REFERENCES

1. Arrow, K. J. "The Role of Securities in the Optimal Allocation of Risk-Bearing," *Rev. Econ. Stud.*, 1964, pp. 91–96.
2. Borch, K. H. "Economics and Game Theory," *Swed. Jour. Econ.*, 1967, pp. 215–228.
3. ———. "The Economics of Uncertainty," in M. Shubik, ed., *Essays in Mathematical Economics in Honor of Oskar Morgenstern*. Princeton, N. J.: Princeton Unversity Press 1967.

7 Corporate

Investment Decisions

7.1. In this chapter we return to the market valuation model developed in Chapters IV and V in order to examine its implications for the company's financial policy. In other words, we turn to the normative aspects of the valuation model. The discussion will be primarily concerned with the investment decisions of the firm, but we shall also touch upon the related question of the firm's dividend policy.

7.2. It is useful to begin by considering the investment theory of Modigliani and Miller (MM) [5], and to do so we must make clear the role of their risk class assumption. It will be recalled from Chapter IV that, by definition, two firms j and k belong to the same risk class if and only if their gross returns are proportional, i.e., if

$$X_k = \alpha X_j.$$

According to MM, this assumption "plays a strategic role in the rest of the analysis" [5, p. 266]. They set out to analyze investments undertaken by a firm in a given risk class. Now it is clear that if company j undertakes an investment which changes its return from X_j to X'_j, it will remain within the same risk class only if X'_j and X_j are proportional, i.e., if

$$(1) \qquad\qquad X'_j = (1 + \lambda)X_j.$$

The real meaning of the risk class assumption is therefore that the MM analysis is restricted to treatment of investments which change the scale of operations, i.e., which are such that gross return changes by the same percentage in all states of the world. The possibility of classifying different companies according to risk seems of less importance.

We observe that the relationship (1) does not necessarily assume constant returns to scale in investment: an investment increasing return by 2 per cent may well cost more or less than twice an investment increasing return by 1 per cent. The requirement is that the investment be of a strictly non-diversifying kind; it should represent, so to say, a chip off the old block. Obviously, this requirement is rather restrictive. We note in particular that a perfectly riskless investment does not satisfy (1) (unless, of course, X_j is already nonrandom).

In analyzing an investment considered by company j, we have to regard other firms' investments as given independently of the decision of company j. Without this assumption, we are conceptually in a complicated oligopoly situation, but one whose effects on the decision to be made appear as rather second-order.

The theoretical basis for MM's investment analysis is that an investment which increases return by a certain percentage in every state of the world must lead to the same relative increase in the company's market value:

$$v'_j = (1 + \lambda)v_j.$$

There is a pitfall to be avoided here, however. It is obviously true that if two firms, j and k, have proportional returns, i.e., $X_k = \alpha X_j$, then company values stand in the same proportion to each other: $v_k = \alpha v_j$. For a formal demonstration, we recall from Chapter IV that an investor's demand functions were

$$\mathcal{E}[u'_i(Y_i)(X_j - rv_j)] = 0 \qquad\qquad (j = 1, \ldots, n).$$

If these equations include

$$\mathcal{E}[u'_i(Y_i)(X_j - rv_j)] = 0$$

and

$$\mathcal{E}[u'_i(Y_i)(\alpha X_j - rv_k)] = 0$$

they can be consistent only if $v_k = \alpha v_j$. It is now tempting to jump to the conclusion that if a company undertakes an investment which increases its return by a certain percentage in all states of the world, i.e., changes X_j to $X'_j = (1 + \lambda)X_j$, then its value will increase in the same proportion. This, however, is not generally true. Such a proportionality relation can hold only as an approximation. The jth demand function now changes to

$$\mathcal{E}[u_i'(Y_i')((1 + \lambda)X_j - rv_j')] = 0$$

or

$$\mathcal{E}\left[u_i'(Y_i')\left(X_j - r\frac{v_j'}{1 + \lambda}\right)\right] = 0$$

where Y_i' is investor i's final wealth after the investment has been undertaken. If we now had $Y_i' = Y_i$, we would obviously have $v_j'/(1 + \lambda) = v_j$, or $v_j' = (1 + \lambda)v_j$. However, $u_i'(Y_i)$ is not entirely unaffected by changes in returns, since Y_i depends directly on aggregate return $\sum_k X_k$, and this will necessarily change when the return of any one company changes. Therefore, one way of "saving" the MM investment theory is to treat this change as a minor and second-order effect by assuming that the number of firms is so large as to make the changes in marginal utilities negligible. Such an assumption simply serves to define the approximation that is admitted by the proportionality assumption. We shall return to a closer examination of this assumption in a little while.

7.3.   If the proportionality assumption is accepted, the rest of the MM investment theory is quite simple. To illustrate, consider an investment project which costs an amount I to undertake, and which will increase return by 100λ per cent. We shall consider the effect of such an investment on the price per share in the case of both equity and debt financing.

Equity Financing

Assume that the number of shares currently outstanding is n_j, so that the price per share is $P_j = p_j/n_j$. By share issue, the number of shares is increased to n_j'; the new issue thus consists of $n_j' - n_j$ shares, and the issue required to finance the investment must clearly satisfy

$$\frac{p_j'}{n_j'}(n_j' - n_j) = I$$

where p_j'/n_j' is the new equilibrium price per share. By solving for n_j', we obtain the new number of shares as

$$n_j' = \frac{p_j' n_j}{p_j' - I}$$

and thus that the new price per share must satisfy

$$P'_j = \frac{p'_j}{n'_j} = \frac{p'_j - I}{n_j}.$$

The new value of equity will be calculated as

$$\begin{aligned} p'_j &= v'_j - d_j \\ &= (1 + \lambda)v_j - d_j \\ &= p_j + \lambda v_j, \end{aligned}$$

and hence the new price per share as

$$P'_j = \frac{p_j + \lambda v_j - I}{n_j}.$$

Thus, the increase in the price per share, $\Delta P_j = P'_j - P_j$, becomes

(2)
$$\begin{aligned} \Delta P_j &= \frac{p_j + \lambda v_j - I}{n_j} - \frac{p_j}{n_j} \\ &= \frac{\lambda v_j - I}{n_j}. \end{aligned}$$

Debt Financing

With debt financing there is no increase in the number of shares, hence $n'_j = n_j$. On the other hand, the debt level increases to

$$d'_j = d_j + I$$

so that the new market value of equity will be calculated as

$$\begin{aligned} p'_j &= (1 + \lambda)v_j - d_j - I \\ &= p_j + \lambda v_j - I \end{aligned}$$

and hence the increase in the price per share as

$$\begin{aligned} \Delta P_j &= \frac{p'_j}{n'_j} - \frac{p_j}{n_j} \\ &= \frac{p_j + \lambda v_j - I}{n_j} - \frac{p_j}{n_j} \\ &= \frac{\lambda v_j - I}{n_j}. \end{aligned}$$

We therefore see that, as expected, the effect of the investment on share prices is the same under both forms of financing. The investment will be considered acceptable only if it serves to raise the price per share, i.e., is such that $\Delta P_j \geq 0$. The critierion for accepting the investment is thus that

$$(3) \qquad \lambda v_j \geq I$$

which quite simply says that the increase in total company value must exceed the cost of the investment.

Alternatively, we can write the investment criterion in the form

$$(4) \qquad \frac{\lambda \mu_j}{\lambda} \geq \rho_j$$

where $\rho_j \equiv \mu_j / v_j$. Here ρ_j is the company's expected rate of return before the investment, and is therefore the company's *cost of capital* as defined by MM. On the LHS we have the expected rate of return of the proposed investment, and the condition for accepting the investment is thus that its expected rate of return exceeds the cost of capital. This is the MM Proposition III. Written alternatively as $\lambda \mu_j / \rho_j \geq I$, the condition is that its expected return discounted at the firm's cost of capital exceeds the amount invested.

As an example, consider a company which initially has a share value of 750 and a debt level of 250, and thus a total value of 1000. The company has the opportunity to make an investment which will increase its return by 25 per cent in all states of the world. Basing its calculations on the proportionality assumption, it will expect its total value to rise to 1250, and it follows that, regardless of the method of financing, the investment will be accepted as long as its cost is less than 250. Suppose the cost of the investment is 200 and the number of shares currently outstanding is 100, each with a price of 7.50. From (2) we can calculate that the price per share will rise by .50 to 8.00. That this is correct proceeds from the fact that at this price the company has to sell 25 new shares to raise the necessary capital, thus increasing the total number of shares to 125. Since the debt level remains the same, the new value of the equity will be 1000, which gives a price per share of 8.00. If, instead, the investment were to be debt financed, the new value of equity would be calculated as $1250 - 450 = 800$, or a price per share of 8.00.

7.4. The MM analysis is not trivial, but since it can handle only very special types of investments, its applicability is severely limited. By means of the explicit market valuation formula

$$v_j = \frac{1}{r}(\mu_j - Rb_j)$$

derived in Chapter IV we should be able to remedy this deficiency, since such a formula puts us in a position to analyze investments with completely arbitrary return characteristics. It should be pointed out, though, that this increased generality with respect to the nature of investments is not obtained without concessions. Our valuation model depends on the assumption that investors choose mean-variance efficient portfolios, whereas no such assumption is required for the MM model. Thus, the price we pay is decreased generality with respect to investors' preferences. However, as we have argued earlier, this price is probably quite low, since investors are likely to choose portfolios which, for all practical purposes, are close enough to efficiency, no matter what their preferences.

Assume now that company j has the opportunity of investing an amount I which will generate a return represented by the random variable Z. Denote the expected return by μ_z, the variance by σ_{zz}, and the covariances with the returns of existing companies (including company j) by σ_{zk}. We also have to regard other firms' investments as given independently of the decision of company j. If the investment is undertaken, gross return will be the variable

$$X'_j = X_j + Z,$$

and it is easily verified that

$$\mu'_j = \mu_j + \mu_z$$

$$\sigma'_{jk} = \begin{cases} \sigma_{jk} + \sigma_{zk} & \text{for } k \neq j \\ \sigma_{jj} + 2\sigma_{zj} + \sigma_{zz} & \text{for } k = j. \end{cases}$$

The new risk measure for the company is therefore

$$b'_j = b_j + b_z$$

where $b_z = \sum_k \sigma_{zk} + \sigma_{zj} + \sigma_{zz}$. b_z represents the increase in company j's risk measure caused by the undertaking of the investment, and may therefore be referred to as the risk measure of the investment itself. Note, however, that because of the appearance of the extra σ_{zj} term, b_z is *not* the same for all companies.

Substituting μ'_j and b'_j into the market valuation formula, we obtain the new value of the company as

$$(5) \qquad v'_j = \frac{1}{r}[(\mu_j + \mu_z) - R(b_j + b_z)]$$

$$= v_j + \frac{1}{r}(\mu_z - Rb_z).$$

Thus, the increase in company value caused by the investment is determined by the same expression as the company value itself, using the mean and the risk measure of the increase in gross return. However, implicit in this statement is the assumption that the market risk aversion factor R will not change as a result of the investment. But R is not entirely unaffected by a change in company return. For the case of quadratic utility functions, we recall that R depends directly on expected aggregate return $\sum_k \mu_k$, and this will clearly change when the expected return of any one company changes. In general, risk aversion will vary with the level of returns, so that strict constancy will not be observed. This, of course, is a problem similar to the one encountered in connection with the proportionality relationship in the MM analysis, and it is natural to make an assumption similar to the one we made there: the number of firms is so large that a change in the return of any one of them does not appreciably affect the market risk aversion factor.

   7.5.   We consider again the effect of undertaking the investment on the price per share with both equity and debt financing.

Equity Financing

   It follows from (5) that the new value of equity becomes

$$p'_j = p_j + \frac{1}{r}(\mu_z - Rb_z)$$

while the new number of shares is given, as before, by

$$n'_j = \frac{p'_j n_j}{p'_j - I},$$

so that the new price per share is

$$P'_j = \frac{p'_j - I}{n_j}.$$

The change in the price per share is then given by

(6) $$\Delta P_j = \frac{p_j + \frac{1}{r}(\mu_z - Rb_z) - I}{n_j} - \frac{p_j}{n_j}$$

$$= \frac{\frac{1}{r}(\mu_z - Rb_z) - I}{n_j}.$$

Debt Financing

In this case the new value of equity becomes

$$p'_j = p_j + \frac{1}{r}(\mu_z - Rb_z) - I$$

while $n'_j = n_j$; thus the change in the price per share is

$$(7) \qquad \Delta P_j = \frac{p_j + \frac{1}{r}(\mu_z - Rb_z) - I}{n_j} - \frac{p_j}{n_j}$$

$$= \frac{\frac{1}{r}(\mu_z - Rb_z) - I}{n_j}.$$

Again we find the method of financing to be irrelevant, and under either form the investment is acceptable if and only if

$$(8) \qquad \frac{1}{r}(\mu_z - Rb_z) \geq I$$

or, equivalently, if

$$(9) \qquad \mu_z - rI \geq Rb_z.$$

In this form, the investment criterion requires, in addition to μ_z and b_z, an estimate of the market risk aversion factor. However, such an estimate is, at least in principle, quite easily available. Using currently available data on the firm's activity, R can be calculated from the market valuation formula as

$$R = \frac{\mu_j - rv_j}{b_j}.$$

Thus (assuming $b_z > 0$) the investment criterion can be written

$$(10) \qquad \frac{\mu_z - rI}{b_z} \geq \frac{\mu_j - rv_j}{b_j}.$$

Again we have, on the RHS, objective data on the firm's current activities—its expected return net of interest cost divided by its current risk measure. On the LHS we have corresponding information on the proposed investment—expected net return divided by its own risk measure. Since the criterion is independent of the method of financing, we can, by defining $\Delta v_j = v'_j - v_j$ as the change in total company value, write the investment criterion generally as

$$\Delta v_j - I \geq 0,$$

without worrying whether I is debt or equity financed.

7.6.   We shall illustrate the relations above by a simple numerical example.

Assume that the economy consists of two companies whose gross earnings in two equally probable states of the world (1 and 2) are given by

		State	
Company	*1*		*2*
1	100		200
2	80		120

We can here compute

$$\mu_1 = 150$$
$$\sigma_{11} = 2500$$
$$\sigma_{12} = 1000$$

and consequently

$$b_1 = 3500.$$

Suppose the market value for company 1 is $v_1 = 125$, and that the risk free interest rate is 6 per cent. From this we may conclude that the risk aversion factor R has the value

$$R = \frac{150 - 1.06(125)}{3500} = .005$$

Assume now that company 1 considers an investment estimated to give a return of 30 in state 1 and 50 in state 2. Notice that this investment is not of the MM type. The expected return is $\mu_z = 40$, and for the covariance terms we find

$$\sigma_{z1} = 500$$
$$\sigma_{z2} = 200$$
$$\sigma_{zz} = 100$$

so that the project's risk measure is

$$b_z = \sum_k \sigma_{zk} + \sigma_{z1} + \sigma_{zz}$$
$$= (500 + 200) + 500 + 100 = 1300$$

Substituting these values in (8), the condition for accepting the project is that

$$I \le \frac{1}{1.06}[40 - .005(1300)] = 31.6.$$

We therefore see that while the preinvestment expected rate of return for the company was 20 per cent, it requires an expected rate of return on the proposed investment of at least 26.5 per cent.

To emphasize the importance of the stochastic dependence between the return on the project and the company's preinvestment return, let us suppose the project had a return of 50 in state 1 and 30 in state 2, thus being negatively correlated with X_1. We clearly have $\mu_z = 40$ and $\sigma_{zz} = 100$ as before, but we now have

$$\sigma_{z1} = -500$$
$$\sigma_{z2} = -200$$

and consequently

$$b_z = -1100$$

so that the investment criterion becomes

$$I \le \frac{1}{1.06}[40 - .005(-1100)] = 42.9.$$

A marginal investment in this case would have a *negative* expected rate of return, but because of the negative correlation, would still not be unprofitable.

7.7. Before examining further some properties of our investment criterion, we shall see what light the market valuation formula may shed on the proportionality assumption of the MM investment theory.

When, as a result of undertaking an investment, company return changes from X_j to $X'_j = (1 + \lambda)X_j$, it is easy to see that the new expected return is

$$\mu'_j = (1 + \lambda)\mu_j,$$

while for the covariance terms we have

$$\sigma'_{jk} = \begin{cases} (1 + \lambda)\sigma_{jk} & \text{for } k \ne j \\ (1 + \lambda)^2\sigma_{jj} & \text{for } k = j. \end{cases}$$

This has the important implication that the company's risk measure does *not* change in the same proportion as return, but rather to

$$b'_j = (1 + \lambda)b_j + \lambda(1 + \lambda)\sigma_{jj}.$$

Thus we always have $b'_j \geq (1 + \lambda)b_j$. It is now clear that, because of the non-proportional change in b_j, the proportionality relation for company value will also be destroyed; instead of getting $v'_j = (1 + \lambda)v_j$, we obtain

$$v'_j = (1 + \lambda)v_j - \frac{1}{r}R'\lambda(1 + \lambda)\sigma_{jj},$$

where R' is the postinvestment value of R. In other words, the difference between the true change in company value and the change implied by the proportionality assumption comes about because of the nonproportional change in the company's risk measure b_j. Thus, calculations based on the proportionality assumption always overestimate the increase in company value. Another way of expressing this is to say that the firm faces a downward sloping demand shedule for its securities. A company with uncertain return is in a way similar to the traditional monopolistic competitor simply because shares in different companies are not perfect substitutes for each other. The difference is that this cannot be said to represent any lack of perfect competition in the capital market.

   A numerical illustration may be useful to explain the differences involved, so we return to the example given in Chapter IV (p. 73) based on quadratic utility functions. In this example we had computed $b_1 = 3/8$, $b_2 = 5/16$, $R = 4/15$ with the resulting equilibrium values $v_1 = 2/5$, $v_2 = 7/6$. Assume now that company 2 undertakes an investment which increases its return by 10 per cent in all three states of the world. The company's expected return is then $\mu'_2 = 11/8$, while the new covariance matrix becomes

$$\begin{pmatrix} \dfrac{1}{4} & \dfrac{11}{80} \\ \dfrac{11}{80} & \dfrac{363}{1600} \end{pmatrix}$$

so that $b'_1 = 31/80$, $b'_2 = 583/1600$. For the new value of R we obtain 8/29, which is larger than the old value of 4/5; this, of course, is because quadratic utility functions exhibit increasing risk aversion. With this the new equilibrium values become

$$v_1 = \frac{114}{290}, \qquad v_2 = \frac{7392}{5800}.$$

To facilitate comparisons, we express all values of company 2 in units of

1/6000, and obtain the following results:

Value before investment	7000
Actual value after investment	7647
Value after investment based on proportionality assumption	7700
Value after investment based on correct $b_2' = 583/1600$ but unchanged $R = 4/15$	7667

7.8. What seems to be the basic problem is the definition of what we mean when we characterize the firm as a "price taker." The proportionality assumption of the MM investment theory can be considered as an assumption of a rather crude sort of price taking behavior, while a more sophisticated firm would recognize the nonproportional change in b_j but still act as a price taker with respect to R. In many ways, the latter conception of the firm seems the more attractive.

For one thing, the ability to separate changes in b_j corresponds to an ability to distinguish between "general market forces" represented by R, on which the firm may quite realistically believe it has no influence, and the unique characteristics of its own shares.

Another reason why the proportionality assumption is undesirable shall be explained more precisely in the next chapter, but its relevance in the present context should be pointed out. If an investment opportunity is characterized by constant or increasing stochastic returns to scale, and the firm calculates on the basis of the proportionality assumption, then no finite equilibrium investment level exists. This is parallel to the inconsistency between nondecreasing returns to scale and perfect competition in traditional market theory.

The last, but perhaps most important, argument in favor of the assumption that firms act as price takers with respect to R is connected with the extension of the analysis to investments which are not of the nondiversifying MM type. When a firm undertakes an investment with a return pattern different from its current return, it does not simply produce "more of the same," and the proportionality assumption simply becomes meaningless. Furthermore, in the context of our market model, it seems that the only sensible way of specifying price taking behavior is with respect to the market risk aversion factor R.

7.9. We noted earlier that the MM analysis was not applicable to a perfectly riskless investment. For a riskless investment we have, of course, $b_z = 0$. We then see directly from (8) above that the investment criterion in this case is

$$(10) \qquad\qquad \frac{\mu_z}{r} \geq I$$

(where μ_z stands for the certain return of the investment). Thus, perhaps not surprisingly, the appropriate rate for discounting the return of a riskless investment is the riskless interest rate.

To illustrate, suppose a wholly equity financed company has current expected earnings of 1200, its riskless borrowing rate is 4 per cent, and its current share value is 1000. This must imply that the risk correction term, Rb_j, equals 160, since

$$\frac{1}{1.04}(1200 - 160) = 1000.$$

Assume now that management discovers an investment opportunity which will require an outlay of 100 and which is considered capable of yielding an 8 per cent return with certainty. Suppose further the investment is to be financed by borrowing. The new expected return will be $\mu'_j = 1308$, with no change in the risk correction term, so that the new value of the firm becomes

$$v'_j = \frac{1}{1.04}(1308 - 160) = 1103.79.$$

The net increase in equity value is therefore 3.79, thus making the investment opportunity a profitable one.

7.10. In this section we turn to a consideration of some of the problems involved in the practical application of our rules for determining whether a proposed investment should be accepted.

We have already considered two cases in which the question of practical implementation should be fairly straightforward: riskless investment, where the choice is made on the basis of net present value using the riskless discount rate, and nondiversifying, or strictly scale-changing, investments, where, if one accepts the proportionality assumption, the choice is made on the basis of expected net present value using the firm's cost of capital, as defined, for discounting. A substantial number of real world investment proposals may fall into either of these categories, particularly relatively small and "everyday" proposals where decision making is largely decentralized. It is comforting to know that fairly simple decision critieria will do for such investments.

Many of the largest and most important investment projects are neither riskless nor nondiversifying, however, and in such cases we should attempt to apply the more general criterion (9). The criterion is admittedly quite complex, and it is not at all clear how we might go about estimating the variables involved. This is particularly true of the risk terms b_z and R. So even though we may be willing to spend effort on collecting data and making estimates, we need some practical guide on the procedure to follow.

Also for this problem, the "simplified model" of Sharpe, discussed in Chapter III, seems very useful, and should probably, in spite of the somewhat restrictive or even inconsistent assumptions of the model, give as reliable estimates as any other procedure.

Define first $X = \sum_j X_j$ as aggregate return, and let $E = \mathcal{E}(X)$ and $V = \text{Var}(X)$. Also, let $W = \sum_j v_j$. From the market valuation formula we have

$$\mu_j - rv_j = Rb_j.$$

Summing over j and solving for R gives

$$R = \frac{E - rW}{V}.$$

The risk measure of the investment was defined as

$$b_z = \sum_k \sigma_{zk} + \sigma_{zj} + \sigma_{zz}.$$

Here we note that the first term is equal to the covariance between Z and X, so we can write

$$b_z = \text{Cov}(Z, X) + \sigma_{zj} + \sigma_{zz}.$$

Assume now that the return of the investment can be decomposed as in the Sharpe model, i.e., as

$$Z = \alpha + \beta X + Q$$

where α and β are parameters to be estimated, and Q is an independent random variable with $\mathcal{E}(Q) = 0$. Thus, $\mu_z = \alpha + \beta E$, so that $Z - \mu_z = \beta(X - E) + Q$. We then have

$$\begin{aligned} \text{Cov}(Z, X) &= \mathcal{E}(Z - \mu_z)(X - E) \\ &= \mathcal{E}[\beta(X - E)^2 + Q(X - E)] \\ &= \beta V \end{aligned}$$

because of the independence of Q. As for σ_{zz}, we have

$$\begin{aligned} \sigma_{zz} &= \mathcal{E}(Z - \mu_z)^2 \\ &= \mathcal{E}[\beta(X - E) + Q]^2 \\ &= \beta^2 V + \text{Var}(Q) \end{aligned}$$

since Q has zero mean.

Suppose now that a similar decomposition can be made of X_j:

$$X_j = \alpha_j + \beta_j X + Q_j$$

so that $X_j - \mu_j = \beta_j(X - E) + Q_j$. We then have

$$\sigma_{zj} = \mathcal{E}(Z - \mu_z)(X_j - \mu_j)$$
$$= \mathcal{E}[\beta(X - E) + Q][\beta_j(X - E) + Q_j]$$
$$= \beta\beta_j V.$$

Collecting the results now obtained we get

$$b_z = \beta V + \beta\beta_j V + \beta^2 V + \mathrm{Var}\,(Q)$$
$$= \beta(1 + \beta_j + \beta)V + \mathrm{Var}\,(Q)$$

and thus

$$Rb_z = (E - rW)\left[\beta(1 + \beta_j + \beta) + \frac{\mathrm{Var}\,(Q)}{V}\right],$$

which is the RHS of (9).

Thus, to obtain an estimate of the correction term for risk, we need estimates of only five parameters: E, β, β_j, $\mathrm{Var}(Q)$, and V. As mentioned earlier, β_j can probably be quite routinely estimated from time series data by least-squares regression on $X_j = \alpha_j + \beta_j X$, where X is taken as an index of aggregate gross earnings. Further, estimates of E and V should be obtainable from various econometric forecasting models. The remaining difficulty is the estimation of β and $\mathrm{Var}(Q)$ in the relation $Z = \alpha + \beta X + Q$. These estimates will probably have to be made on an ad hoc basis, and little of general interest can be said about the procedures that might be followed in doing so. However, the decomposition of Z into one part that moves with the rest of the economy and another which is independent and unique to the project under consideration should provide a useful frame of reference for the collection and systematic analysis of data on the project.

7.11. In Chapter V we showed that the market valuation formula also held if there was a positive probability of default, and the firm therefore had to pay interest on its bonds above the riskless rate. It then follows that the investment criterion is independent of the firm's debt level and borrowing rate. This fact has some surprising consequences. For example, we noted that the appropriate interest rate for discounting a perfectly riskless investment was the riskless rate. Now suppose the riskless rate is 4 per cent, but the firm, because of its default chances, faces a borrowing rate of 10 per cent. If an investment opportunity arises which will yield 8 per cent with certainty, our model asserts that it should be perfectly acceptable to the stockholders for the firm to go ahead and borrow in order to undertake such an investment. The explanation of this seeming paradox is that although the current borrowing rate is 10 per cent, the effective *marginal* borrowing rate is considerably lower, in fact, lower than 4 per cent.

In section 5.7 we derived an expression for the firm's contractual interest rate in the case where its gross return had a two-point distribution independently of other firms; it was given by

$$(11) \qquad r_j = (a + 1)r - a\frac{\beta}{d_j}$$

where

$$a = \frac{p[1 + R(1 - p)(\alpha - \beta)]}{(1 - p)[1 - Rp(\alpha - \beta)]}.$$

We shall use this model to illustrate the ideas involved.

As a numerical example, we considered a company with gross yield $\beta = 1200$ with probability $p = .1$ or $\alpha = 2400$, a debt level $d_j = 1500$, a riskless interest rate $r = 1.04$, and a risk aversion factor $R = 1/1080$. We then calculated $a = .25$, and thus

$$r_j = 1.25(1.04) - .25\frac{1200}{1500} = 1.10,$$

i.e., an equilibrium contractual interest rate of 10 per cent. Suppose now that this firm finds an opportunity to invest 250 with a certain return of 8 per cent and considers the possibility of financing the investment by borrowing. If this is done, the relevant new parameter values would become

$$\alpha' = 2400 + 1.08(250) = 2670$$
$$\beta' = 1200 + 1.08(250) = 1470$$
$$d'_j = 1500 + 250 = 1750.$$

Since the coefficient a depends only on the range $\alpha - \beta$ of the probability distribution, it remains unchanged; the new contractual borrowing rate would therefore become

$$r'_j = 1.25(1.04) - .25\frac{1470}{1750} = 1.09,$$

i.e., a rate of 9 per cent. This is still higher than the investment return of 8 per cent, but the important point is that this rate applies to *all* debt, not only the increase caused by the investment. Thus, before the investment the company was under obligation to pay to bondholders the amount $r_jd_j = 1.10(1500) = 1650$, while the figure now is $r'_jd'_j = 1.09(1750) = 1907.50$. This represents an increase of 257.50, which is precisely 3 per cent more than the 250. Thus, the effective marginal borrowing rate is 3 per cent, and it is then not surprising that the proposed investment should be considered profitable. To achieve this effect, the company must convert its old loan of 1500 with 10 per cent interest into a new loan of 1750 with 9 per cent interest. The market should accept this because when the investment is undertaken, the loss to bondholders in case of default is reduced (from 300 to 280), and this reduction is reflected in the market's valuation of the bonds as a decrease in the contractual interest rate.

To see these relationships in more general form, let I be the amount invested and p the certain rate of return. As noted, the coefficient a remains unchanged, since both α and β change by the same amount if the investment is undertaken, while the other new parameter values are

$$\beta' = \beta + pI$$
$$d'_j = d_j + I$$

so that r'_j is given by

$$r'_j = (a + 1)r + a\,\frac{\beta + pI}{d_j + I}.$$

The contractual repayment is then

$$r'_j d'_j = (a + 1)r(d_j + I) - a(\beta + pI)$$
$$= r_j d_j + (a + 1)rI - apI$$

and the increase in the contractual repayment thus

$$\Delta r_j d_j \equiv r'_j d'_j - r_j d_j$$
$$= [(a + 1)r - ap]I.$$

The effective marginal borrowing rate is therefore

$$\frac{\Delta r_j d_j}{I} = (a + 1)r - ap.$$

It would seem natural to expect that an investment was considered acceptable if this rate were below the return on the investment, i.e., if

$$(a + 1)r - ap < p.$$

But this inequality reduces simply to

$$p > r,$$

which is just the criterion implied by (10).

We note finally that in the numerical example we found that the effective marginal borrowing rate was below the riskless interest rate, i.e.,

$$(a + 1)r - a\rho < r.$$

We see that this generally holds as long as the return on the investment is higher than the interest rate, i.e., as long as $\rho > r$.

7.12.   The preceding discussion shows that it is time to face more squarely the concept of cost of capital and its role in the firm's capital budgeting decisions. The first thing to note is that there does not seem to be any agreed upon definition of *the* cost of capital. Presumably the cost of capital is some sort of interest rate which is to be used as a cutoff rate or discount rate for proposed investments. Precisely how it is to be measured or used are more controversial questions, although it is noteworthy that many discussions seem to assume that the cost of capital is a characteristic determined by the capital structure of the firm, and thus can be measured independently of its use for investment decision making purposes.

On the basis of the theory presented above, it must be concluded that many of these ideas have to be rejected. Indeed, we shall argue that any concept of cost of capital resembling the traditional one is, in general, meaningless, or, even if it can be construed, is probably going to have properties quite different from those of the traditional view. In a way, such a conclusion is not really surprising. If we accept value maximization as the general (but nonoperational) formulation of company objectives, the task of financial theory is to derive its operational implications. If we start with a completely open mind as to what the criterion for undertaking an investment may look like, there is no reason to believe that it must be of the simple-minded form suggested by traditional theory: that the project's net cash flow discounted at some interest rate should be positive.

First, since capital structure is of no consequence for valuation, it follows that the criterion for undertaking an investment is independent of both existing and proposed financing arrangements. Hence, even if the investment criterion could be expressed in terms of a cost of capital formulation, that cost would be independent of capital structure and, in particular, of the difference between the firm's borrowing rate and the riskless rate. It would be difficult to find a discussion of the cost of capital concept which did not assume that the higher the interest paid on a firm's debt, the higher its cost of capital, because of its default chances. In other words, traditional financial theory suggests that certain investment projects exist which may be profitable if the borrowing rate is 5 per cent, but which should be rejected if, as a result of a high debt level, the rate is 10 per cent (given that the riskless rate is the same). Such a view as we have seen, is mistaken.

Second, the criterion for undertaking a project is, in general, unique to that particular project, although for projects within certain classes the criterion may be the same even though the projects are not strictly identical. The latter is clearly the case for projects of the nondiversifying MM type. If attention is restricted exclusively to this type of investment, so that the firm always stays within the same risk class, it would certainly be meaningful to speak of the firm's cost of capital. But this exceptional case is clearly best suited to illustrate the rather limited generality of a cost of capital concept.

When arbitrary investment return patterns are admitted, it may still be possible to express the investment criterion in terms of a cutoff rate of return; specifically, it is seen that (4) can be rewritten as

$$\frac{\mu_z}{I} \geq r + \frac{Rb_z}{I}$$

where the LHS is the project's expected rate of return. However, the cutoff rate, given by the expression on the RHS, is clearly not the same for all projects, so it is not possible or meaningful to speak of *the* cost of capital for the firm independently of the project being considered.

The foregoing does not mean that the profitability of an investment depends on nothing but the return characteristics of the investment itself. This is because the risk measure b_z associated with the project is, in general, different for different firms. However, this difference has nothing to do with the capital structure of the company, but depends only on its return characteristics prior to the investment. Thus, we may say that whether an investment should be undertaken or not depends on its return characteristics *relative* to the company's existing return characteristics. For example, the lower the correlation between the investment's return and the company's existing return, the more desirable (other things being equal) is the project. A closer analysis of how the investment criterion depends on the preinvestment return, and thus differs for different firms, will lead to some interesting conclusions.

7.13. In order to make a comparison of the investment criteria of two different companies meaningful, we have to assume that the return Z of the project under consideration is independent of which firm undertakes it. In the derivation above of the investment criterion for any given firm, no such assumption was implied. Now, however, we consider only projects which are "technologically independent" of the sponsoring firm in the sense that the expected return μ_z and all covariance terms σ_{zj} are the same regardless of which firm undertakes them. Without this assumption we could not really say that a given project is the "same" for both firms, and hence could not speak meaningfully of different firms' investment criteria for the "same" project.

With this assumption, we can write the investment criteria for companies j and k as

$$\Delta v_j - I = \frac{1}{r}[\mu_z - R(\sum_s \sigma_{zs} + \sigma_{zj} + \sigma_{zz})] - I \geq 0,$$

$$\Delta v_k - I = \frac{1}{r}[\mu_z - R(\sum_s \sigma_{zs} + \sigma_{zk} + \sigma_{zz})] - I \geq 0.$$

Writing the criterion for company j as $I \leq K$, the criterion for company k can then be expressed as

$$I \leq K - \frac{R}{r}(\sigma_{zk} - \sigma_{zj}).$$

Thus, as already noted, if $\sigma_{zk} > \sigma_{zj}$, the criterion will be stricter for company k than for company j.

One interesting implication of this relationship is the following. Consider two firms which are identical except for their scales of operation, i.e., which belong to the same risk class so that $X_k = \alpha X_j$. Specifically, assume that $\alpha > 1$, meaning that company k is the larger of two. It then follows that $\sigma_{zk} = \alpha \sigma_{zj}$, implying that the investment criterion for company k becomes

$$I \leq K - \frac{R}{r}(\alpha - 1)\sigma_{zj}.$$

Assuming positive correlation, this formulation implies that *the criterion is stricter the larger the company*. At first thought, one would probably expect a small company to be more reluctant than a big company to undertake a given risky project, or at any rate that in a perfect capital market with homogeneous expectations, the investment criterion should not depend on which firm undertakes the project. What we have established here is that the marginal effect of investment on company value decreases with its scale of operation. This is again related to the observation, made before, that as a result of varying return patterns, the rate of increase in value decreases with its scale of operation.

7.14. The preceding analysis indicates that an investment undertaken by one firm will affect the values of other firms as well. To see this, consider the effect on the value of company k of an investment made by company j. Obviously, μ_k remains the same as before the investment; the same is true of the variance σ_{kk} and the covariance terms σ_{ks} for $s \neq j$. However, the covariance with company j changes to $\sigma'_{kj} = \sigma_{kj} + \sigma_{zk}$, so that the risk measure is changed to $b'_k = b_k + \sigma_{zk}$. Therefore, there will be a change in v_k equal to

$$\Delta v_k = -\frac{R}{r}\,\sigma_{zk}.$$

Thus, if σ_{zk} is positive, the effect will be a reduction in the value of company k. In other words, the total effect of the increased riskiness caused by the investment is not fully internalized by the firm undertaking it. This would seem to suggest that risk (or, rather, positive correlation) may in some way represent a type of external diseconomy, perhaps similar to the diseconomy arising when one fisherman's catch is adversely affected by an increase in the scale of operation of another. It appears, however, that such an external effect of risky investment is not a true externality in a general equilibrium sense, or at least not welfare-relevant. Rather, it must be categorized as a "pecuniary" externality, as that term has been employed by Scitovsky [8], since it is transmitted through market prices rather than by direct technological dependency among firms.

One firm increasing its output may cause factor prices to increase or output prices to fall, and these price changes may reduce the output and profit of other firms. There are now two possibilities to consider. If the market was originally in equilibrium and no changes in demand or technology have taken place, there is no reason for any firm to increase its output; such a change obviously represents a movement away from equilibrium and therefore has no well defined welfare implications. If, on the other hand, the change is caused by, say, a shift in the firm's production function, then the output change is just the first step in a movement toward a *new* equilibrium position. The price changes caused by such an output change are simply signals to other firms to adjust themselves to changed technological conditions. The external effects of risky investment are clearly of a similar nature. It should be kept in mind that the investment projects with which we are dealing in this chapter are of a "windfall" nature whose undertaking implies a shift from one equilibrium position to another. The next chapter, where we consider determination of the firm's total level of investment, will provide a more meaningful framework for analysis of the efficiency of investment allocation among firms.

7.15.   This concludes our discussion of the corporation's investment policy, and we turn now to an examination of certain aspects of a related decision: the company's dividend policy. Unfortunately, dividend policy has not been very satisfactorily developed from a purely theoretical point of view, and we shall therefore restrict our presentation to an overview of some possible approaches to the problem.

Let us first clear away one possible source of confusion. We shall be concerned with the purely "economical" effects of dividend policy, and not with what may be called the *informational content* of dividend payments. Clearly, declaration of a particular dividend payment is to many investors an important source of information on the economic condition of the company. A high dividend payment may be taken as an indication that the company's prospects are bright; this causes investors to revise their estimates of the probability distribution for earnings, and therefore causes market value to change. This is not to say that a raised dividend payment necessarily results in a rise in share price. There have been instances when companies have declared unchanged or even increased dividends in order to camouflage poor earnings, but the inside story somehow got on the front page of the *Wall Street Journal*, with the result that the dividend had nothing like the effect planned. This is basically the kind of situation we shall assume to prevail, in which investors are fully informed on the real economic situation of the firm. But because of the informational content of dividends, many writers suggest that, whether dividend payments are economically relevant or not, companies are well advised to exercise considerable care in changing existing dividend policy.

7.16.   Even with the assumption of full information of the true condition of companies, there appears to be considerable disagreement in the literature on the role of dividend policy. One simple classification of the views might be into those that hold that dividend policy does not matter, and those that believe that it does matter. Let us examine some of the various schools of thought within each category.

One point of view is associated mainly with traditional economic theory and is based on certain assumptions of equilibrium in the economy. The reasoning is that if the economy is in a state of static equilibrium, the marginal rate of return is the same in all investment activities, and is furthermore equal to investors' marginal rate of time preference. This applies to investment opportunities available to both firms and individuals. In that case, to take a dollar away from investment in one activity and pay it out as dividend to an investor for consumption or for investment elsewhere brings neither loss nor gain. Therefore, the dividend payment is a matter of indifference.

There are at least two serious problems with this view. First, few, if any, economies are actually in a state of static equilibrium; there is continuous development and technological change, with new investment opportunities arising and old ones becoming obsolete. Second, the theory is based on the assumption of complete certainty. If investment yields are stochastic, as they are in practice, and individuals differ in their risk aversion, it is not at all obvious that dividend policy is irrelevant even if investment equilibrium prevails. Hence the theory, even if valid on its own assumption, seems of limited practical interest.

A different theory in support of the basic irrelevance of dividend policy is associated mainly with Miller and Modigliani [4]. Their treatment of this issue has also been subject to controversy, apparently based on failure to recognize the rather strong *ceteris paribus* assumptions on which the theory is based. Once these are realized, the reasoning seems straightforward.

The crucial assumption in their argument is that the dividend payment does not affect the economic activity carried out by the firm; in other words, the dividend payment is assumed to come from a source which leaves the probability distribution for company return X_j unchanged. This requirement obviously implies two things. First, the value v_j of the firm remains unchanged after the dividend payment. Second, the amount of the dividend payment must be financed from the outside (either by borrowing or share sale), since otherwise the resources available to the firm would be reduced and thus change X_j.

Denote by D the amount of dividend paid, and let p'_j and d'_j be the value of equity and the debt level, respectively, after the dividend payment. Since v_j does not change, we clearly have

$$p'_j = v_j - d'_j.$$

Suppose now that the dividend payment is to be financed by borrowing; this means that $d'_j = d_j + D$, so that

$$p'_j = v_j - d_j - D$$

or

$$p'_j = p_j - D.$$

In other words, the value of the shares decreases by precisely the amount of the dividend payment. But this must mean that the dividend is a matter of indifference to stockholders: having a share worth $45 and a dividend check for $5 cannot, at least on a rational basis, be considered either worse or better than having a share worth $50. Of course, companies which reduce dividends will frequently get complaints from widows and orphans who claim they need the money for living expenses. The answer to this is that they can continue their consumption level by selling off the appropriate number of shares and still maintain the value of their holdings.

If, instead, new shares are issued, increasing the number of outstanding shares from n_j to n'_j, it is easily verified that the new value per share is reduced to

$$\frac{p'_j}{n'_j} = \frac{p_j}{n_j} - \frac{D}{n'_j},$$

i.e., by the dividend per share. Hence the method of financing is, as before, irrelevant.

7.17. It is probably fair to say again that even though the theory as outlined may be valid on its own assumptions, these assumptions seem to eliminate from consideration some aspects of the dividend policy problem that would appear to be important in the real world. First, a dividend payment typically *does* represent a loss of resources for the firm, and the problem is therefore likely to be viewed as one of balancing the dividend payment now against future earnings opportunities foregone. Second, the company may be concerned about building or maintaining its financial security, and may therefore wish to retain earnings in order to reduce the chances of ruin. Neither of these aspects can be captured within the framework of a single-period model. In discussing a few possible approaches, we first present a model considered by Borch [1] which, in spite of its extreme simplicity or even artificiality, brings out the "financial security" aspect of the dividend policy.

The model assumes a company which has a given initial capital and which in each period makes a profit X which is a stochastic variable. The company is further assumed to operate under the following conditions:

1. If the capital becomes negative at the end of a period, the company is ruined and goes out of bussiness.
2. If at the end of a period the capital exceeds an amount Z, the excess is paid out as dividend.

The fact that the probability distribution for profits is assumed to be the same in all periods implies that the profits earned are not reinvested to earn any yield; presumably, retained earnings are set aside in a noninterest bearing account with the sole purpose of providing a reserve against future losses (negative profits). The dividend policy defined above is obviously of a very special kind, and it is natural to take Z as a decision variable to be chosen in accordance with the company's objectives. Specifically, Borch considers two variables of possible concern to the firm's owners or management: *the expected time until ruin*, $D(Z)$, and *the expected present value of future dividend payments*, $V(Z)$. We shall not go into the derivation of the expressions for these variables, as the mathematics involved is fairly advanced. However, the main results are that $D(Z)$ is monotonically increasing (in fact, progressively increasing), and that $V(Z)$ is first increasing and then decreasing, and therefore implies a maximizing value of Z.

Let us for the moment assume that the objective of the firm is to maximize $V(Z)$. By choosing a high value of Z (relative to initial capital), it is clear that it will take a long time before the first dividend payments are made. On the other hand, such a policy will also serve to extend the duration of the dividend payments, once they are started, far into the future. Conversely, a low value of Z promises early dividend payments, but increases the chances of early ruin. The maximizing value of Z clearly reflects the balancing of these two effects.

The stationarity assumptions of the model, both with respect to succesive profit distributions and the dividend policy itself, reduce its attractiveness somewhat, although it would seem possible to introduce certain growth elements to reflect investment return on retained earnings. The mathematics of such a formulation would be rather forbidding, however. Another, and theoretically more troublesome, problem is the fomulation of the company's objective. In this book we have postulated value maximization as the appropriate objective, and it is by no means clear that this objective is equivalent to maximization of the expected present value of future dividend payments. What seems to be called for is a model relating dividend policy to market value. As noted earlier, various attempts at constructing such models do not, at least to this writer, seem very satisfactory from a purely theoretical point of view.

7.18. Most discussions of the effect of dividend policy start by postulating as self-evident that the value of a share derives ultimately from the dividend payments it promises to pay in the future. If it was known with absolute certainty that a share would never ever pay a single penny, nobody in his right mind would be willing to pay anything for it (we include as a dividend any redemption value of the share in case of dissolution of the company). The theorist then faces three different problems.

First, he has to specify the nature of the investment opportunities available to the firm, so that the effect of retained earnings at one point in time on the probability distributions for earnings in later periods can be described. Such a specification essentially serves to define the set of feasible dividend payments. A large number of assumptions, basically of a technological nature, can be made concerning these relationships, and the theorist will usually have to restrict his attention to a few typical cases. This in itself will clearly restrict the generality of the resulting theory.

The second problem is to specify the *form* that the dividend policy should take. Since the funds available for dividend payments and other relevant variables are unknown, it is impossible to specify a sequence of dividend payments $D_1, D_2, \ldots, D_n, \ldots$ once and for all. Rather, a general policy must be specified, relating the dividend payment to the values of certain specified parameters. We have already seen an example of one such policy in Borch's model; it was of the form, "If capital exceeds Z, pay the excess as dividends." A policy having an entirely different form would be, "If profits are negative, pay nothing; otherwise pay B per cent of it as dividends." Obviously there are a great many forms that the dividend policy can take, and the theorist again has to concentrate on a few that seem appealing. In each case there will be one or more parameters (such as Z and B in the examples), the values of which have to be specified in an optimal fashion. The problem is that even with such optimal parameter values, the form of the policy may be suboptimal, and it is generally quite difficult to determine whether some other form of policy (with corresponding optimal parameter values) might not be superior. All this serves to complicate the development of a general theory of the effect of dividend policy.

The third problem is probably the most elusive and difficult to come to grips with, at least on the theoretical level. It concerns the determination of the value of the shares of a company with given investment opportunities for retained earnings, and a specified dividend policy. With a given dividend policy successive dividend payments are represented by a stochastic process, so the problem can be stated as one of determining the market value of a stochastic process.

Most work on this problem is based on the idea that market value is determined as if future dividend payments were discounted to the present by a method which somehow takes the uncertainty about size of payment into account. On the precise nature of the procedure for discounting there seems to be considerable disagreement, however, which is not really surprising, because all the models that have been proposed rest on ad hoc assumptions. The assumptions may seem reasonable enough and perhaps intuitively appealing, but we end up with a kind of my-assumptions-are-more-realistic-than-yours argument. For example, a well known dividend valuation model is that presented by Gordon [2]. His model is based on the hypothesis that investors view receipts which are in the distant future as more uncertain than current or imminent receipts; he then postulates a discount factor that, in a rather complex way, is made to increase with time. Now the various assumptions may seem quite reasonable, but since they are not *derived* from more fundamental properties of equilibrium in the security markets, they leave the theorist somewhat uneasy.

7.19.   Two alternative approaches to the dividend valuation problem seem possible. One, and the theoretically more attractive, would be to derive the valuation of shares from a general equilibrium model in which investors' demand relations explicitly recognize the multiperiod nature of their portfoilo choices. In such a formulation, the immediate portfolio decision would have to be seen as the first in a sequence of portfolio (and possibly also consumption) decisions, and would therefore depend on parameters describing the firms' dividend policies. A general equilibrium model with these characteristics should then be able to yield certain relationships between share prices and dividend policies.

Promising as research along these lines may seem, it is certain to meet with difficulties. For one thing, work on multiperiod portfolio policies is still in its infancy, and concrete results have been obtained only for special utility functions [3, 6, 7]. It is not clearly established what role mean-variance efficiency, so crucial to the theory developed in this book, may play in a multi-period context, and existing multiperiod portfolio theory is not formulated in a way which explicitly incorporates dividend policies. But, of course, problems are there in order to be solved.

   Another approach would be to apply our one-period valuation formula in a step-by-step fashion so as to get an evaluation of a multiperiod stream of payments. To give an indication of how this might be accomplished, we shall consider an extremely simplified example.

   Consider a firm which in any period t earns a random return Y_t per dollar of capital C_t, where the Y_t's are independently and identically distributed (independently also of earnings of other firms) with mean μ and variance σ^2. Suppose further that the firm follows a policy of retaining a fraction ρ of its earnings so that the fraction $1 - \rho$ is paid as dividends. The retention rate is to be considered as the firm's decision variable. Assume finally that the firm has no debt. We shall consider the valuation of such a firm for an horizon of two periods, i.e., after two periods we assume all capital to be paid out as dividend.

   With initial capital C_1 the earnings in period 1 are $X_1 = C_1 Y_1$. The first dividend payment is thus $(1 - \rho)C_1 Y_1$, with a resulting new level of capital $C_2 = C_1(1 + \rho Y_1)$. Earnings in period 2 are thus $X_2 = C_1(1 + \rho Y_1)Y_2$, so that the final capital level is $C_3 = C_1(1 + \rho Y_1)(1 + Y_2)$. Consider now the value V_2 of the company at the beginning of period 2. At this time, V_2 can be determined on the basis of our valuation formula as

$$V_2 = \frac{1}{r}[\mathcal{E}(C_3) - RVar(C_3)]$$

$$= \frac{1}{r}[C_1(1 + \rho Y_1)(1 + \mu) - RC_1^2(1 + \rho Y_1)^2\sigma^2].$$

The mean and variance of C_3 are here taken with respect to Y_2 only, because at the beginning of period 2, Y_1 is no longer random. Note, however, that *as of the beginning of period 1, V_2 is random*, depending as it does on the then uncertain Y_1. At the same time, of course, the dividend for period 1 is also random. As of the beginning of period 1, the end-of-period value of the firm is therefore the random variable

$$Z_1 = (1 - \rho)C_1 Y_1 + V_2.$$

We can now once more apply our market valuation formula to obtain the current value of the firm as

$$V_1 = \frac{1}{r}[\mathcal{E}(Z_1) - RVar(Z_1)].$$

We shall not evaluate the expectation and variance here, since the expressions get very complicated. It is clear, however, that we shall in the end obtain V_1 expressed in terms of the given parameters, say as

$$V_1 = f_2(\mu, \sigma^2, r, \rho, R, C_1)$$

where the subscript to f indicates the length of the horizon. We could now conceivably proceed to consider a similar derivation of V_1 for an arbitrary horizon of t periods (possibly through some recursive relation between f_t and f_{t+1}), and ultimately arrive at *the* valuation formula by letting t tend to infinity. Hopefully, this limiting process would accomplish some simplifications in the formula for the finite horizon case.

We shall not pursue these ideas further, but only offer them as a suggestion of what might conceivably be done. One obvious problem with the approach as suggested is that it leads to mathematical expressions which, although elementary, appear forbiddingly complicated.

REFERENCES

1. Borch, K. H. *The Economics of Uncertainty.* Princeton, N. J.: Princeton University Press, 1968.
2. Gordon, M. J. *The Investment, Financing and Valuation of the Corporation.* Homewood, Ill.: Richard D. Irwin 1962.
3. Hakansson, N. H. "Optimal Investment and Consumption Strategies under Risk for a Class of Utility Functions," *Econometrica,* 1970, pp. 587–607.
4. Miller, M. H., and F. Modigliani. "Dividend Policy, Growth, and the Valuation of Shares," *Jour. Bus.,* 1961, pp. 411–433.
5. Modigliani, F., and M. H. Miller. "The Cost of Capital, Corporation Finance, and the Theory of Investment," *Amer. Econ. Rev.,* 1958, pp. 261–297.
6. Mossin, J. "Optimal Multiperiod Portfolio Policies," *Jour. Bus.,* 1968, pp. 215–229.
7. Samuelson, P. A. "Lifetime Portfolio Selection by Dynamic Stochastic Programming," *Rev. Econ. Stat.,* 1969, pp. 239–246.
8. Scitovsky, T. "Two Concepts of External Economics," *Jour. Pol. Econ.,* 1954, pp. 143–151.

8 Distribution
of Investment Capital

8.1. Even though the investment theory presented in the last chapter provides a number of useful insights, it was basically *partial* in nature. That is, the analysis took as given the probability distributions for the firms' preinvestment returns, and on this basis considered criteria for accepting small, or marginal, changes in those returns. We did not ask how or why firms arrived at the investment level or capitalization they happened to have, or whether these variables represented "optimal" or "equilibrium" values. Thus, the analysis could be compared with one of the classical models of commodity exchange in which we ask the question: What would be the value of a marginal increase in the given supply of some commodity? We do not ask why the supply is what it is in the first place.

8.2. In this chapter we shall broaden the scope of the analysis by considering the simultaneous determination of the firms' overall level of investment and the allocation of claims to the resulting return distributions among individual investors. Such an extension is similar to the extension of a model of pure exchange of commodities to a model of equilibrium of both production *and* exchange. More specifically, rather than taking the probability distributions for returns X_j as given, we now conceive of each firm as having available to it an *investment opportunity*, or a *stochastic production* *function*

(1) $X_j(\theta) = \phi_j(I_j, \theta)$

where $X_j(\theta)$ is the firm's output in state of the world θ given as a function of its level of investment I_j.

The difference between the two formulations is perhaps seen more clearly by recalling our example of each firm being a farm, organized—or to be organized—as a corporation. In the pure exchange model of Chapter IV, the farms had already, at the time of trading, effected their investment (planting of its land) as well as financing (share sale and borrowing). Thus, the supply of shares and corporate bonds were given data. Trading of these securities was among investors only, and did *not* represent any source of investment funds for the companies. In the model considered now, however, we examine the trading and contracting at an earlier point in time: before the planting of the land. The firms here place *new issues* of bonds and/or shares on the market, the proceeds of which are used for investment. We shall consider, in turn, both pure debt financing, pure equity financing, and mixed financing. The prospectus of the firm offering securities for sale is basically a description of its production function (1).

8.3.   A complete model of saving and investment would include determination of investors' choices between present and future consumption. Such a model would explain not only the distribution of savings among different investment opportunities, but also the amount of savings itself. It would actually be fairly straightforward to formulate such a model in general terms. It would include specification of investor preferences in terms of a two-variable utility function:

$$U_i = \mathcal{E}[u_i(C_{i0}, C_{i1})]$$

where C_{i0} and C_{i1} are present and future consumption. His budget constraint would include both present consumption and amounts invested in the various securities available; future consumption would consist of the (random) returns from these securities.

We shall, however, abstain from this opportunity for generalization. The generalized model would complicate the analysis without throwing any additional light on the problems with which we are mainly concerned, namely, the distribution of investment among firms. Thus, we shall take as given both the total amount of resources available for investment and the risk-free interest rate (both of which would be endogenously determined in a complete saving-investment model).

8.4.   Since we measure both investment and return on investment in the same units, it may be useful to think of this as a single, physical commodity such as "corn," which serves as both a factor of production and a consumption good. This is intended only as a help in fixing ideas. We could equally well think of inputs and outputs as measured in terms of "generalized purchasing power," such as money, with fixed relative prices among commodities.

8.5. We shall first consider the situation in which investment is financed exclusively by bond issues. That is, equity ownership is already established by share issues prior to the current contracting, so the supplies of shares are given data and do not represent current sources of investment capital for the firms. In terms of our example, we can think of the farms as having acquired their land some time in the past (and exogenously to our model); the trading now will only determine the amount of seed to be planted, together with the allocation of claims to output among investors. To begin with, we shall assume that default risk is never present for any firm. This model has been discussed in general form by Diamond [1], and our initial analysis follows his closely.

Investors' initial endowments consist of ownership of stocks of input, $\bar{s}_i$, and the values of initial shareholdings, $\sum_j \bar{z}_{ij} p_j$. Thus, initial wealth is defined by

$$W_i = \bar{s}_i + \sum_j \bar{z}_{ij} p_j.$$

By assumption, the initial allocation is such that $\sum_i \bar{z}_{ij} = 1$ for all j. Define $s = \sum_i \bar{s}_i$ as the given total amount of investment (savings) available. Then total private wealth is

$$(2) \qquad \sum_i W_i = s + \sum_j p_j.$$

In allocating his wealth, the investor is, as before, faced by the budget condition

$$(3) \qquad W_i = m_i + \sum_j z_{ij} p_j,$$

where z_{ij} are his shareholdings after the trading and m_i his net riskless investment, which may consist of either financial lending or investment in a riskless physical investment opportunity. The final allocation must clearly satisfy

$$(4) \qquad \sum_i z_{ij} = 1 \qquad\qquad (j = 1, \dots, n)$$

which is seen to imply, in view of (2), that

$$(5) \qquad \sum_i m_i = s.$$

Note that when physical investment is introduced, it need not necessarily be true that $\sum_j d_j = \sum_i m_i$, since part of the available investment funds may be allocated to one or more riskless physical investment opportunities. Such a condition would actually overdetermine the model.

8.6. With pure debt financing, the investment undertaken by firm j will be just equal to the amount of debt issued, d_j, so that output will be described by

$$X_j(\theta) = \phi_j(d_j, \theta).$$

Thus, after firms have announced their choices of the d_j, the probability distributions for the X_j, and hence also for return to shareholders, $X_j - rd_j$, will be known. Investor i's demand for shares are therefore, as before, given by the conditions

(6) $\mathcal{E}[u_i'(Y_i)(X_j - rv_j)] = 0$ $(j = 1, \ldots, n)$

where

$$Y_i = rW_i + \sum_j z_{ij}(X_j - rv_j)$$

and

$$v_j = p_j + d_j.$$

8.7. Following Diamond, we shall first study the case in which the production function is *decomposable*, i.e., can be written in the form

$$X_j(\theta) = \phi_j(d_j, \theta) = g_j(d_j)h_j(\theta).$$

This means that variation in input level causes output to change by the same percentage in all states of the world; this represents an extension of the "non-diversifying" investment opportunities of the Modigliani-Miller theory. Thus, changing input by the factor k causes output to change to

$$X_j'(\theta) = g_j(kd_j)h_j(\theta)$$
$$= \frac{g_j(kd_j)}{g_j(d_j)} X_j(\theta).$$

If the firm bases its calculations on the proportionality assumption discussed in the last chapter, it will assume that a given percentage change in output in all states of the world will change its market value by the same percentage. Therefore, at the input level d_j, with a corresponding market value of v_j, it would calculate the market value at the input level kd_j as

$$v_j' = \frac{g_j(kd_j)}{g_j(d_j)} v_j.$$

The corresponding value of equity would be

$$p'_j = \frac{g_j(kd_j)}{g_j(d_j)} v_j - kd_j$$

and the firm would consider it optimal to invest to the point where the derivative of p'_j with respect to k equals zero:

(7)
$$\frac{dp'_j}{dk} = \frac{g'_j(kd_j)d_j}{g_j(d_j)} v_j - d_j = 0.$$

At the optimal value of d_j, this derivative is evaluated at $k = 1$, so the equilibrium condition for investment becomes

$$\frac{g'_j(d_j)}{g_j(d_j)} v_j = 1,$$

or, more instructively,

(8)
$$\frac{g_j(d_j)}{g'_j(d_j)} - d_j = p_j.$$

As it stands, this condition is not particularly useful for the firm for planning or decision making. The share price p_j is a variable which is determined in the market for any given values of the d_j, and is therefore not observable ex ante. Rather, the rule allows the company to confirm, after investment has been effected, whether these plans were indeed optimal. That is, the rule doesn't tell you how to get to the top but how to recognize it when you're there.

Alternatively, we can consider the relation (8) as the firm's *demand schedule* for borrowing, given as a function of its share price. If a "market manager" announces a set of share prices, firms can use (8) to calculate their bond issues, while individuals, thus knowing the values of the v_j, can calculate from (6) and (3) their desired stock and bond holdings. If the values of the z_{ij}, m_i, and d_j so chosen satisfy the market clearing conditions (4) and (5), an equilibrium position has been attained; otherwise the market manager announces a new set of share prices and the process is repeated.

8.8.   We note that the demand schedule (8) makes sense only if the production function exhibits (stochastic) decreasing returns to scale, i.e., is such that $g''_j < 0$. This is most easily seen from the second order condition for a maximum of p_j:

$$\frac{d^2 p'_j}{dk^2} = \frac{g''_j(kd_j)d_j^2}{g_j(d_j)} v_j < 0,$$

which clearly requires $g''_j < 0$. Under constant returns to scale ($g''_j = 0$) and, *a fortiori*, under increasing returns to scale ($g''_j > 0$), the derivative

(7) is clearly everywhere nonnegative, implying that for no value of p_j does a finite value of d_j maximizing share value exist.

So what if one or more firms happen to have a production function with nondecreasing returns to scale? Does no equilibrium exist, or is the model inconsistent? In a sense, the model *is* inconsistent, and the inconsistency is precisely the same as that encountered in classical market theory: acting as price takers, firms with nondecreasing returns to scale would expand output to the extent that they would influence prices, and thus not be price takers after all. We shall see that when the proportionality assumption is abandoned no such problems need arise.

8.9.   Assuming decreasing returns to scale, it is easy to determine the slope of the demand functions (8). By implicit differentiation we obtain

$$\frac{dd_j}{dp_j} = -\frac{(g'_j)^2}{g_j g''_j},$$

which must be positive. This is both a natural and in some sense "desirable" result. Suppose the market manager had announced a set of prices p_j which were predominantly lower than the equilibirum prices. This would mean that investors' demand for shares would exceed the given supply, while their demand for bonds would be below the supply offered by firms at those share prices. Then, by raising the p_j, *both* demand and supply would move closer to the equilibrium levels.

8.10.   Is the allocation of available investment capital resulting from (8) Pareto-optimal? To examine this, assume a situation in which the demand functions (6) and (8) and the market clearing conditions (4) [implying (5)] hold, and consider a reallocation dz_{ij}, dm_i, and dd_j. Such a reallocation must clearly satisfy

$$\sum_i dz_{ij} = \sum_i dm_i = 0.$$

From the definition of Y_i it follows that

$$dY_i = r\,dm_i + \sum_j (X_j - rd_j)\,dz_{ij} + \sum_j z_{ij}\left(\frac{\partial X_j}{\partial d_j} - r\right)dd_j,$$

so that the changes in expected utilities are

(9) $dU_i = \mathcal{E}[u'_i(Y_i)dY_i]$

$\qquad\qquad = r\mathcal{E}[u'_i(Y_i)]dm_i + \sum_j \mathcal{E}[u'_i(Y_i)(X_j - rd_j)]\,dz_{ij}$

$\qquad\qquad\quad + \sum_j z_{ij}\mathcal{E}\left[u'_i(Y_i)\left(\frac{\partial X_j}{\partial d_j} - r\right)\right]dd_j.$

Now, with a decomposable production function $X_j(\theta) = g_j(d_j)h_j(\theta)$ we have

$$\frac{\partial X_j(\theta)}{\partial d_j} = g'_j(d_j)h_j(\theta)$$

$$= \frac{g'_j(d_j)}{g_j(d_j)} X_j(\theta).$$

Substituting for g'_j/g_j, we can write (8) as

$$\frac{\partial X_j(\theta)}{\partial d_j} = \frac{X_j(\theta)}{v_j}$$

and we then have

$$\mathcal{E}\left[u'_i(Y_i)\left(\frac{\partial X_j}{\partial d_j} - r\right)\right] = \mathcal{E}\left[u'_i(Y_i)\left(\frac{X_j}{v_j} - r\right)\right]$$

$$= \frac{1}{v_j} \mathcal{E}[u'_i(Y_i)(X_j - rv_j)]$$

which, by (6), is equal to zero. Thus, each term in the last sum in (9) is zero. From (6) it also follows that the first two terms in (9) reduce to

$$dU_i = r\mathcal{E}[u'_i(Y_i)](dm_i + \sum_j p_j dz_{ij}).$$

Writing $\alpha_i = 1/r\mathcal{E}[u'_i(Y_i)]$ as in Chapter VI, it then follows from the market clearing conditions that

$$\sum_i \alpha_i dU_i = 0.$$

Since the α_i are positive, the dU_i cannot all be positive; hence the allocation based on (8) is Pareto-optimal. Before examining the significance of this result, let us consider the problem of determining an optimal level of investment in the more general case of a nondecomposable production function.

8.11. Dropping the decomposability assumption, it remains true that the firm wants to carry investment to the point where the derivative of share value with respect to input level is zero. However, actual application of such a rule depends upon our conception of the firm as a price taker. As was shown in Chapter VII, the analogue to the proportionality assumption in the case of a nondecomposable production function was the assumption that the firm behaves as if it considered itself incapable of influencing investors' marginal utility. Let us consider the investment level which would, under this assumption, be considered optimal.

From equations (6) it follows that equilibrium share prices must satisfy

(10)
$$p_j = \frac{\mathcal{E}[u_i'(Y_i)X_j]}{r\mathcal{E}[u_i'(Y_i)]} - d_j.$$

We can then, in principle, write the conditions for the determination of the d_j as

$$\frac{dp_j}{dd_j} = \frac{\mathcal{E}\left[u_i'(Y_i)\dfrac{\partial X_j}{\partial d_j}\right]}{r\mathcal{E}[u_i'(Y_i)]} - 1 = 0,$$

or, more simply,

(11)
$$\mathcal{E}\left[u_i'(Y_i)\left(\frac{\partial X_j}{\partial d_j} - r\right)\right] = 0.$$

In differentiating, we have here considered Y_i as independent of d_j.

The condition (11) is of even less help to the firm in its decision making than the condition (8). Since it involves investors' (unobservable) preferences rather than just variables observable in the market, it is completely nonoperational as an investment criterion. It is a purely formal representation of a condition that is satisfied when the firm, by some sort of divine guidance, has chosen what it considers an optimal value of d_j.

The main significance of condition (11) in the present context is that it implies a Pareto-optimal distribution of investment among firms. When (11) is satisfied, each term in the last sum in (9) is zero; equations (4) and (6) then guarantee Pareto-optimality.

8.12.   We have now established that, in the cases of decomposable and nondecomposable production functions, respectively, equations (8) and (11) implied Pareto-optimality. These equations were in turn conditions for optimal investment levels under the given specification of the firms as price takers. The point to be made now is that the values of the d_j implied by these conditions are *not the values that in fact maximize share prices*. As a result, we cannot conclude (at least not without serious qualifications) that maximization of share values leads to an efficient allocation of investment.

The reason for this is simply that equations (8) or (11) were based on the proportionality assumption and the assumption of constant marginal utilities, respectively, and these assumptions do not correctly describe the firm's position in the market. We saw in Chapter VII that calculations based on the proportionality assumption always overestimated increases in share value, and therefore lead to investment levels larger than those which maximize share values. In the general case it can be shown that the "correct" condition for maximization of p_j [i.e., the condition obtained by differentiation of (10) taking the dependence of Y_i on d_j into account] is that

$$\varepsilon\left[u_i'(Y_i)\left(\frac{\partial X_j}{\partial d_j} - r\right)\right] = -\varepsilon\left[u_i''(Y_i)z_{ij}\left(\frac{\partial X_j}{\partial d_j} - r\right)(X_j - rv_j)\right]$$

and if this condition is satisfied we no longer achieve Pareto-optimality.

As we have pointed out on several occasions, the presence of uncertainty introduces a monopolistic element in the demand for a firm's securities. With this in mind, we see that our conclusions have a direct parallel in classical market theory: If a seller in fact faces a downward sloping demand curve but *believes* that he cannot influence price, he will consider it in his best interest to choose an output level where price equals marginal cost, and this we know is a requirement for Pareto-optimality. This output is larger than that which would actually maximize his profit, however.

One possible way of summing up the situation is to say that share value maximization as a company objective is not inconsistent with the achievement of Pareto-optimality, but that a necessary additional condition for Pareto-optimality is that firms consider themselves price takers as specified.

8.13. There are at least two reasons why equation (11) is ineffectual as a rule for competitive production in the general case of a nondecomposable production function. First, we did not make full use of the general equilibrium conditions, since the market clearing conditions were not invoked in the course of the analysis. Second, we made no specification of investors' preferences. In the preceding chapter we demonstrated how the market valuation formula derived on the assumptions that investors choose mean-variance efficient portfolios, and that demand equals supply for all securities, could be used to derive operational decision criteria for investments with arbitrary probability distributions for yield. In the same way we shall show by examples how the same relation can make it possible to determine an optimal level of investment for a firm with a completely arbitrary production function. This requires, as we argued in Chapter VII, that we abandon the proportionality assumption as a definition of the firm as a price taker, and assume that the firm considers the market risk aversion factor R as given while recognizing the relationship between its investment level and its risk measure b_j.

Except for the numerical determination of R, the market valuation formula derived in Chapter IV remains valid for the model treated here, since the demand functions (6) and market clearing conditions (4) are identical. The difference, of course, is now that μ_j and b_j are no longer exogenously given data, but depend functionally on the investment decisions.

To illustrate the determination of R, consider the case in which all investors have quadratic utility functions $\mu_i = Y_i - c_i Y_i^2$. On the RHS of equation (8) in Chapter IV we substituted $\sum_i W_i = \sum_j p_j$, while we now have from (2) that $\sum_i W_i = s + \sum_j p_j$. Using this relationship, we find that R will be determined as

$$R = \frac{1}{c - rs - \sum_j \mu_j}$$

where $c = \sum_i 1/2c_i$ (c, r, and s are given market parameters).

The general procedure for determining the firm's optimal level of investment is in principle quite simple. Since the probability distribution for return depends on the amount d_j invested, the first- and second-order moments can be considered as direct functions of d_j; taking these relations into account, we can then find the optimality conditions by straightforward differentiation. Thus, from the market valuation formula we have that the share value of company j is

(12) $$p_j = \frac{1}{r}(\mu_j - Rb_j) - d_j.$$

Differentiating with respect to d_j then gives the optimality condition

$$\frac{dp_j}{dd_j} = \frac{1}{r}\left(\frac{d\mu_j}{dd_j} - R\frac{db_j}{dd_j}\right) - 1 = 0,$$

or, rearranging,

(13) $$\frac{d\mu_j}{dd_j} = r + R\frac{db_j}{dd_j}.$$

Thus, investment should be carried to the point where the expected return on the last dollar invested is equal to the interest rate plus a correction term for risk. The second-order condition for a maximum is that

$$\frac{d^2\mu_j}{dd_j^2} < R\frac{d^2b_j}{dd_j^2}$$

8.14. We shall illustrate the application of the investment rule (13) by some specific examples.

First, consider the case of a decomposable production function, $X_j(\theta) = g_j(d_j)h_j(\theta)$. Assume further that the return of company j is distributed independently of the return of other firms; this means that b_j is just equal to the variance of the firm's return. Let $\mathcal{E}[h_j(\theta)] = \mu$ and $\mathrm{Var}[h_j(\theta)] = \sigma^2$; we then have

$$\mu_j = g_j(d_j)\mu$$
$$b_j = [g_j(d_j)]^2\sigma^2$$

and consequently

$$\frac{d\mu_j}{dd_j} = g'_j(d_j)\mu$$

$$\frac{db_j}{dd_j} = 2g_j(d_j)\,g'_j(d_j)\sigma^2.$$

Inserting these terms in (13) and rearranging, we can write the investment rule in the form

(14) $$g'_j(d_j)[\mu - 2Rg_j(d_j)\sigma^2] = r.$$

It is interesting to compare this rule with that obtained under the proportionality assumption from (8). Assuming the market valuation formula to hold, (8) would imply the condition

$$\frac{g'_j(d_j)}{g_j(d_j)} \cdot \frac{1}{r}[g_j(d_j)\mu - R(g_j(d_j))^2\sigma^2] = 1$$

or

(15) $$g'_j(d_j)[\mu - Rg_j(d_j)\sigma^2] = r.$$

Thus, under the proportionality assumption the optimal d_j would appear as if computed from (14), but using a risk aversion factor only one-half the value of R. This would obviously lead to a higher value of d_j and a correspondingly reduced value for p_j.

For the special case of constant returns to scale, i.e., $g_j(d_j) = d_j$, (14) can be solved for the optimal investment level in explicit form as

$$d_j = \frac{\mu - r}{2R\sigma^2}$$

with a corresponding maximal value of equity of

$$p_j = \frac{(\mu - r)^2}{4rR\sigma^2}.$$

Suppose, for example, a one-period return on every dollar invested of either zero or 20 per cent with equal probability. Then $\mu = 1.1$ and $\sigma^2 = .01$; if the interest rate is 5 per cent ($r = 1.05$) and $R = 1/1000$, the optimal investment is $d_j = 2500$ and the corresponding share value $p_j = 57.14$. If instead we think of a perpetual yield with the same distribution for return per period and the same interest rate, we have $\mu = .1$, $\sigma^2 = .01$, $r = .05$, and thus the same $d_j = 2500$, while the share value becomes $p_j = 1250$.

As an example of a nondecomposable production function, consider the following:

$$X_j(\theta) = 2d_j - \frac{1}{500\theta} d_j^2 \qquad (\theta = 1, 2)$$

with probability 1/2 for each value of θ. Notice that with this production function maximum return is attained for the input levels 500 and 1000, respectively, in states 1 and 2. We find here

$$\mu_j = 2d_j - \frac{3}{2000} d_j^2; \qquad \frac{d\mu_j}{dd_j} = 2 - \frac{3}{1000} d_j$$

$$b_j = \frac{1}{4,000,000} d_j^4; \qquad \frac{db_j}{dd_j} = \frac{1}{1,000,000} d_j^3.$$

Substituting the derivatives in (13) (and still assuming $R = 1/1000$, $r = 1.05$), we obtain the third-degree equation

$$d_j^3 + 3,000,000 d_j = 950,000,000$$

with the approximate solution $d_j = 307$. The corresponding maximum share price is then roughly $p_j = 141$.

8.15.   The investment levels determined in these two examples represent optimal decisions for the firm. But since we just took the price of risk, R, as a given magnitude, they are not necessarily general equilibrium solutions. That is, we did not derive the simultaneous market determination of R. To illustrate the nature of the complete general equilibrium solution, we shall consider the first example of a constant returns to scale production function in the case where there is only a single firm (which we nevertheless must assume acts as a price taker with respect to R). To be able to determine R explicitly, we shall also assume that all investors have quadratic utility functions so that R is given by

$$R = \frac{1}{c - rs - \mu_j}.$$

With $d_j = (\mu - r)/2R\sigma^2$, we have $\mu_j = \mu d_j = \mu(\mu - r)/2R\sigma^2$; hence R must satisfy

$$R = \frac{1}{c - rs - \dfrac{\mu(\mu - r)}{2R\sigma^2}}.$$

The solution is

$$R = \frac{2\sigma^2 + \mu(\mu - r)}{2\sigma^2(c - rs)}$$

and the corresponding solution for d_j is

$$d_j = \frac{(\mu - r)(c - rs)}{2\sigma^2 + \mu(\mu - r)}.$$

In the numerical example used above we therefore get

$$R = \frac{3.75}{(c - 1.05s)}$$

$$d_j = \frac{2}{3}(c - 1.05s).$$

The value $R = 1/1000$ is therefore consistent with a value for $c - rs$ of 3750.

8.16.   Thus far we have disregarded the possibility of default and the possible effect of such a contingency on the firm's investment decision. This neglect may seem inconsistent, since in the numerical example with constant returns to scale there is always a possibility of default. If investment should result in a zero return, there will be insufficient funds for servicing the debt. (This will be the case at any level of investment, not only the optimal one.)

We shall contend, however, that our analysis is correct and that the investment rule (13) is valid even if it should imply nonnegative default chances. The argument is actually quite simple. The investment rule (13) is derived directly on the basis of the market valuation formula (10), and we demonstrated in Chapter V that this relationship holds even in the presence of default risk. Here we consider μ_j and b_j as functions of the level of investment, while in that chapter we took them as given data, but this in no way invalidates the relationship expressed by the market valuation formula. It then follows that the input level which satisfies (13) is optimal regardless of whether it implies an amount of debt that results in a positive probability of default.

When investment is all debt financed, the Modigliani-Miller Proposition I is no longer valid: when the amount of debt, and therefore the level of investment, is changed, the total value of the firm is also changed. For example, with constant returns to scale, company value is given by

$$v_j = \frac{1}{r}(\mu d_j - R\sigma^2 d_j^2)$$

and is thus a quadratic function in the amount of debt. But such a relationship is clearly unrelated to the question of the validity of the market valuation formula.

8.17.   We have given a fairly detailed account of the determination of the firm's optimal level of investment when investment funds are acquired exclusively by debt issue, and we now turn to a consideration of some of the problems arising when investment funds are provided by the sale of shares. In Chapter VII, where we considered criteria for marginal investments, i.e., for movements from one equilibrium position to another, we found that the method of financing did not affect the investment criterion. In a model including simultaneous determination of input levels and pricing and allocation of securities, however, the situation is drastically changed.

In the case of debt financing, we had to take the supply of shares as given prior to the trading, so that an investor's initial wealth consisted of both stocks of input and the value of his shareholdings. Now, however, we deal with a model involving *initial financing* of the companies, so that investors' starting wealth consists exclusively of stocks of input. In our farm allegory, we start with the organization of ownership of land, not with just the planting of that land. Thus, within our model, the difference between debt and equity financing is not a simple difference in the method of financing, but also implies a difference in what is being financed or the way in which production and distribution are organized. A comparison of investment level determination in the two versions of the model is therefore not really meaningful.

8.18.   The most important difference between investment models with debt and equity financing is that in the latter *the firm is not in a position to exercise discretion in the determination of its level of investment*. It can do nothing but passively adapt investment to what the market is willing to supply.

Suppose, for example, that the promotors of a given investment opportunity announce plans to invest ten million dollars in that opportunity by selling a million shares at a price of ten dollars per share. Once the amount of investment is known, the shape of the probability distribution for return from the project is known, and to this yield distribution there would correspond a particular market value of the shares. However, that price need not necessarily be ten dollars! It might be nine dollars, but in that case it would be impossible for the firm to carry out its original plans. In general, there exists only one level of investment which generates a probability distribution for return such that the market value of the firm becomes precisely equal to that amount of investment. The firm's management has no independent choice but to accept this amount; it is the only decision capable of being implemented, and the only decision consistent with equilibrium.

From the market valuation formula we can see quite explicitly why firms are unable to determine their input levels independently. With no debt the share value is given by

(16) $$p_j = \frac{1}{r}[\mu_j(p_j) - Rb_j(p_j)],$$

where we have emphasized that μ_j and b_j depend directly on the amount invested, p_j, by using a functional notation. This relation represents an equation in p_j which must be satisfied in equilibrium. No optimization is (or can be) involved in the determination of p_j.

8.19.   To illustrate the determination of p_j by (16), we shall consider the two examples of production functions given in paragraph 8.14. With a constant returns to scale production function, where $\mu_j = \mu p_j$ and $b_j = \sigma^2 p_j^2$, (16) takes the form

$$p_j = \frac{1}{r}(\mu p_j - R\sigma^2 p_j^2).$$

The solution for p_j is

$$p_j = \frac{\mu - r}{R\sigma^2},$$

which is the equilibrium investment level. Suppose again that $\mu = 1.1$, $r = 1.05$, $\sigma^2 = .01$, and $R = 1/1000$; then $p_j = 5000$. With this investment expected yield is $\mu_j = 5500$ and the risk measure $b_j = 250,000$, so that the market value of the firm becomes

$$p_j = \frac{1}{1.05}\left(5500 - \frac{250,000}{1000}\right) = 5000.$$

The last calculation illustrates the dual roles of p_j as a measure of both the market value of the probability distribution for return and the level of input itself.

For the numerical example with a decreasing return to scale production function, insertion of μ_j and b_j in (16) leads to the condition

$$p_j^3 + 6,000,000 p_j = 3,800,000,000$$

with the approximate solution $p_j = 598$. With this investment level we find $\mu_j = 660$ and $b_j = 31,970$; the corresponding market value is therefore

$$p_j = \frac{1}{1.05}\left(660 - \frac{31,970}{1000}\right) = 598.$$

8.20.   The idea that equity financing precludes independent decision making for the firm may require some reflection in order to be appreciated.

The real world counterpart to the financing and investment activities considered in our analysis is clearly the offering of stock to the public for the first time. In such a situation it seems to be in agreement with the casual observation that there is little the prospective company's management can do but sit back and wait for the final price of the issue. True, the firm has to "decide" on an initial offering price in the preliminary prospectus, but this is basically only an estimate of what investors in the aggregate will be willing to pay. The role of *underwriters* is to provide expertise and serve as a means of communication between investors and the company. If the company were in a position to make a decision that would stick, there would be no need for such middlemen.

The fact that the share prices and the allocation of investment capital among firms are determined in the market rather than by the firms themselves represents a kind of *investor sovereignty* which may have a certain appeal on ethical grounds (whatever that is). After all, it is investors who provide the input and carry the risk, so it seems reasonable that they should be the ultimate judges of how it should be spread.

8.21. However, there is a more significant, but also a more intricate, problem in connection with a model of initial equity financing, and that is the problem of company objectives. Even if it *were* possible for management to influence the proceeds from security issues, how could we formulate sensible criteria for such decisions? There are no "old" stockholders whose interest can be appealed to, hence an objective such as share value maximization makes little sense. Indeed, why should one try to make it as expensive as possible to buy shares in the new firm?

The real problem is not the difficulty in suggesting a reasonable answer to the question of company objectives; the question itself is actually meaningless. A corporation in itself can have no independent objectives; these can emanate only from those who eventually will own an interest in the company, and at the time when the issue is announced no information about such prospective interests is available. An investor may find, in retrospect, that he would have been better off if different financing and investment decisions had been made, but it is evidently impossible to base criteria for initial financing on such considerations. The impossibility of a meaningful formulation of company objectives seems to be the fundamental and inevitable problem with any model where the value of a claim to a share in profits also represents a source of investment capital.

In a discussion of the initial investment and financing of a company, it would seem natural to include more explicitly the role of the "management" or the "promotors" of the new enterprise. We have assumed that such groups play an entirely neutral role, although in actual practice they may represent special interest groups whose objectives may affect the company's investment and financing. However, it seems quite difficult to recognize such phenomena in a formal model, since the form in which such efforts will be rewarded may vary considerably. But it seems clear that such special interests will be present only if the reward is made dependent on the company's earnings. In that case, we are back to a situation basically the same as that in which there are "old" shareholder interests. Such a situation serves only to reinforce the general proposition made above: unless there are groups with "vested interests" in the company, no formulation of criteria for optimal investment or financing is meaningful.

8.22. As long as the amount invested is equal to the total market value of the firm's securities (no vested interests), a model with both debt and equity financing has much the same characteristics as the model with pure equity financing.

First, we still have the problems connected with formulation of relevant criteria for optimal investment and financing arrangements for the firm; as before, there is, at the time of trading, no definable group whose interest in the firm seems a natural target for appeal.

As far as management's *ability* to determine the firm's investment and financing is concerned, the amount of debt can be decided upon arbitrarily. However, the really interesting question is whether management has any possibility of influencing the *total* proceeds from security issues, thus affecting the amount of investment in the enterprise. Here we can generally formulate the main result as follows: If the market is such that the Modigliani-Miller Proposition I (MM I) holds, then the level of investment is determined by the market and cannot be influenced by management action.

This statement may seem self-evident, if not outright tautological. MM I simply says that the total value of the firm depends only on the probability distribution for return and not on its financial mix; since the value of the firm is equal to the amount of investment and hence determines completely the probability distribution for return, there is only one level of investment compatible with equilibrium.

From these considerations it follows that the determination of the d_j is of no particular consequence from the point of view of either individual investors or the market as a whole. We saw in Chapter IV that investors' preferred probability distributions for portfolio return would be the same under alternative levels of debt. Hence they should not, even in retrospect, mind what debt levels were decided upon in the first place. From the point of view of efficiency of market allocation, it is only the distribution of investment among firms that matters, not their financing.

8.23. If the MM I did *not* hold, we would be, conceptually and theoretically, in a rather messy situation, with the firm obtaining different amounts of investment funds at alternative levels of debt. Selection of a particular value of d_j would no longer be unimportant, since these decisions would affect the distribution of investment capital among firms. However, we have not been able to come up with a sensible criterion for firms to employ in their determination of the d_j; the model would therefore be underdetermined in an essential way.

It is difficult to evaluate the practical importance of such a situation. In Chapter V we showed that the MM I holds under extremely general conditions, and that the only reason why MM I might fail to hold would be market imperfections of various sorts. Without a formal analysis of such imperfections (which appears forbiddingly difficult), it is hard to say anything meaningful about the nature of their effects.

8.24.   Before concluding our discussion of initial financing, perhaps some words should be said about its role in financial theory. Is initial financing, from either a practical or a theoretical point of view, such a terribly vital question after all? Some general considerations suggest that perhaps it is not.

In the first place, it may be argued that the question of origin or past history has no direct consequence for today's decisions. Whether we believe that man was created according to Genesis or according to biological evolution makes hardly any difference in our daily conduct of practical affairs. In the same way, the establishment of economic activity, including its financial form, is a matter of historical accident with no immediate bearing on today's decision problems. General Motors is what it is today, and its executives need not know how the company was started in order to perform in the shareholders' interest. It should also be kept in mind that organized financial markets are a relatively recent phenomenon. Existing economic activity may be reorganized in a number of ways, even through formation of new companies, but this does not represent initial financing in the sense discussed here and is, as we have seen, irrelevant from a financial markets point of view.

Even when a new economic activity is started, it is seldom launched as a publicly held corporation. By the time a company goes public—thus making market valuation a meaningful concept—there are important "vested interests" present in the form of the original owners' or founders' shareholdings. In that case, a share issue is no longer initial financing, and we are back to a model like that described in Chapter 7 or the Diamond model.

From considerations such as these it would seem unreasonable to exaggerate the importance of the theoretical problems arising in connection with initial financing in pure form.

REFERENCE

1. Diamond, P. A. "The Role of a Stock Market in a General Equilibrium Model with Technological Uncertainty," *Amer. Econ. Rev.*, 1967, pp. 759–776.